What Time Is the Midnight Buffet?

What Time Is the Midnight Buffet?

✦

Tales from the Cruise Adventure of a Lifetime

chesterh

iUniverse Star
New York Lincoln Shanghai

What Time Is the Midnight Buffet?
Tales from the Cruise Adventure of a Lifetime

iUniverse Star
an iUniverse, Inc. imprint

iUniverse books may be ordered through booksellers or by contacting:

iUniverse
2021 Pine Lake Road, Suite 100
Lincoln, NE 68512
www.iuniverse.com
1-800-Authors (1-800-288-4677)

Cover illustration by Larry Ross
www.larryross.net

ISBN: 978-1-58348-488-3 (pbk)
ISBN: 978-0-595-86327-3 (cloth)
ISBN: 978-0-595-86172-9 (ebk)

Printed in the United States of America

To Kris, of course...

Contents

Foreword

This is a true story. It reflects our experience during our first-ever cruise and does not necessarily mean that yours will be the same—but I hope it is. Some names of individuals mentioned in this book may have been changed to protect their privacy.

Pictures and other materials to accompany the text of this book are available on the Internet (http://book.chesterh.com).

To Cruise or Not to Cruise

It was the kind of early May morning that made me feel like it was worth suffering through six months of New Hampshire winter to experience—simply glorious. To top it off it was Saturday, which meant that we could relax with the newspaper and coffee on the sun porch. No pressure…

My wife, Kris, was looking out the kitchen window as the coffee pot gurgled. She suddenly stiffened and drew a sharp breath. "Oh my God! I can't believe it! You have to see this!" Her tone sent a shiver down my spine, and I expected something bad to be in the backyard—maybe a body.

"What's the matter?' I asked as I bolted to the window, heart racing.

"Look! Over there!"

"What?"

"The wisteria. It's blooming!"

Sure enough, it was. We planted the thing years earlier and it had never produced a single flower. For us, this was a momentous occasion.

"It must be a sign," I said.

"Of what?" Kris asked.

"I dunno…something good."

Later, as we sat on the sun porch admiring the wisteria, the sky darkened to an ominous hue and big wet snowflakes started falling. We sat in silent disbelief as the wisteria and all other signs of spring disappeared under a thick coating of white.

Kris broke the silence. "We ought to go somewhere."

I considered this for a moment before responding. "Like the bookstore?"

"No, I mean for our anniversary." Without the enticement of spring to keep her mind occupied, Kris's thoughts had turned to our upcoming twenty-fifth anniversary.

"Yeah, I guess we should plan something to celebrate. This is a biggie," I said.

"So we should do something special, don't you think?"

"Sure. But what?" I asked.

We are simply not vacation people. I can count our genuine vacations on slightly more than one half of a hand—two trips to Disney World with the kids, and a long weekend in Quebec City. My name is Richard, although nobody calls me that. I've had the nickname "Chester" since childhood, the result of a simple case of mistaken identity. I am an aging computer geek who manages engineering projects for a living. Kris recently became a high school biology teacher after a long stint as an operating room nurse, trading a hard job for an impossible one. Our time away from work is generally spent planting things that never bloom, or going to Kris's parents' lakeside camp in nearby Maine. With a typical summer-time population of fifteen to twenty people, the camp is a raucous place. I am the closest thing to a handyman in the extended family and usually spend my time there fixing things. Not exactly relaxing, but someone has to keep the place from falling down. To me, vacations mean work.

"I don't know what we should do. You decide," said Kris.

"How about the honeymoon suite at the Motel 6 for a whole weekend?"

Kris ignored my attempt to be cute. "Maybe we could go to the Mt. Washington Hotel this summer."

The Mt. Washington Hotel in New Hampshire is a classic Victorian resort in a stunning setting, but I thought that we ought to do something radically different to celebrate a quarter century of legally sanctioned togetherness. "I don't know about the hotel. It's old, and I'd probably spend my time looking for things to fix," I countered. An advertisement in the newspaper triggered an idea. "How about a cruise?"

"That's for old people," Kris replied.

"We are old people, now."

"We're not *that* old. Besides, it must be really expensive."

She had a point there. "OK, I'll check out the hotel."

I logged on to my computer and looked up the offerings at the Mt. Washington Hotel. A deluxe room went for $345–$525 per night, per person. Suites topped out at $1600. No wonder we didn't take vacations.

I reported the results back to Kris, and summed up in two words: "Forget it."

"Wow, that's a whole lot more than I expected," she said. "Oh, well. Let's go somewhere."

"How about the bookstore?"

"Good idea."

We drove through the falling snow to the bookstore. As a defense against the weather, the conversation turned to the time we spent living on St. Thomas in the Virgin Islands. My first job took us to the island in 1977. We married, went to St. Thomas for the honeymoon and stayed for three years.

"I wish we still lived on St. Thomas," said Kris.

The feeling was mutual. "Back to de ship?" I said, mimicking the island accent. It was a phrase we heard countless times during our residency there, as cab drivers mistook us for cruise tourists.

"Ya, mon," Kris answered. "Maybe we *should* look into a cruise. Wouldn't it be nice to go back to St. Thomas on a ship?"

Cruise ships were a central element of life on St. Thomas. Every day, several ships would arrive and disgorge thousands of people onto the dock. Most of those people would head straight downtown to shop in the duty-free stores. Few would venture outside of town, so the vast majority completely missed the beauty of the island. I was always mystified why people would pay dearly to take a slow boat to a shopping mall.

"It would be a new perspective. I've always wondered why people went on those ships. There must be more to it than shopping in exotic places," I said.

"Do you really think we should give it a try?" Kris asked.

"I don't know. What do you think?"

"What if we hate it? I'm not sure if I want to be stuck on a ship with nothing to do all day," she said. I'd heard several people utter that refrain.

"Well, we could always just relax and read."

"I suppose."

"Want me to look into it?" I asked.

"Whatever you think is best, dear. You know I trust your judgment."

I took her answer as an affirmative and decided to go for it.

Barnes & Noble is a fine place to spend time on a snowy day in May. I gravitated to the travel section to find inspiration for the anniversary celebration, and selected two books on cruising: the *Berlitz Guide to Cruising and Cruise Ships*, and, because it seemed fitting, *Cruising for Dummies*.

Back at home, I read both books in short order. Kris was immersed in a paperback, content to leave the research to me. The books made it plain that cruises and cruise lines come in many different flavors—a bewildering array of choices, in fact. This wasn't going to be easy.

I decided I needed to know more, and turned to the Internet. I found dozens of Web sites dedicated to cruising, and many had discussion boards (forums) where people asked and answered questions, wrote trip and ship reviews and posted pictures. After surveying several of these sites, I settled on one that seemed to have more activity and information than most: *www.CruiseCritic.com*. I had to choose a user name to participate in the discussions on CruiseCritic, so I tried "chester." The name was already allocated to someone else, so I added the first letter of my last name and tried "chesterh." That did it—the new identity was all mine.

A lot of the information I found was amusing, but less than helpful. One couple reported that their cruise experience was ruined because iced tea was unavailable between 3:00 and 4:00 p.m. I found lively discussions about the quality of the toilet paper, the effectiveness of the hair dryers, and the absence of proper fish knives, whatever they are. Some cruisers seemed to rate their level of satisfaction by inverse proportion to the wear evident on the ship's carpeting. Others reported having a wonderful time, but beyond the declaration, there was little information to substantiate the claim. People were obviously passionate about cruising, but despite many hours spent reading everything out there, I still couldn't fathom why this was so. What was the real attraction? Other than eating, what did one do all day on a big boat in the middle of nowhere? What was the *feel* of a cruise?

People seemed evenly divided on the value of a private balcony (verandah)—some considered them to be an extravagance since they spent very little time in their cabins, while for others, a verandah was vitally important. I sided with those holding the latter view. In further refining the possibilities, I determined that we should avoid the summer camp feeling of some popular ships, which feature blaring PA systems and hairy leg contests. Peace and quiet should prevail.

Initially, I considered a cruise to Bermuda out of Boston—mainly for convenience. Boston is less than an hour from our home in southern New Hampshire, and since I hate flying, the idea of driving to the dock was attractive. Unfortunately, all of the ships sailing from Boston were older models—built without verandahs.

I was beginning to get discouraged when I happened upon a description of an accommodation called the sky suite, available on a trio of ships operated by Celebrity Cruises. This line had already bubbled to the top of the prospect list due to its reputation for excellent food and service in a laid-back atmosphere. Besides a catchy name, two features of the sky suite stood out. The verandahs were reported to be among the largest at sea, several times the typical size. In addition, suites on Celebrity ships feature butler service. Extravagances to be sure, but I figured that they would improve our chances of enjoying the trip—from essentially none to at least slim.

In a flurry of Internet activity, I found that one of the qualifying ships was sailing 10-day western Caribbean itineraries from Baltimore. I almost got up the nerve to book the trip, but when I checked the pricing, I got cold feet. The Motel 6 option bubbled back to the top of the list.

The following day, Dick, a coworker, came in to my office and sat down. "Any vacation plans this year?" Dick asked.

"Nah. We don't really take vacations," I answered.

"You don't? I sure do. Every year, I make sure to plan a special trip somewhere."

"Ever been on a cruise?"

"No, it just never appealed to me. I don't want to be stuck on a ship with nothing to do all day. We usually go to a nice beach resort. Someplace exotic."

"I was thinking of trying a cruise. It's our twenty-fifth anniversary this year," I said.

"Hey, congratulations. You seem kind of young for a cruise, but I think you should go for it," said Dick.

"I don't know. It's so expensive."

"How much?"

I gave him the figure for the 10-day cruise.

"That's it—for a big anniversary trip? I budget more than that every year for regular vacations," said Dick.

"I've never even spent that much on a car for myself. Granted I never buy anything built in the current decade, but how do you afford it?"

"Hey, I just make a budget and stick to it. You have to reward yourself first. Life is too short."

It was a defining moment for me, and a plan quickly developed in my head. As soon as I got home that night, I booked Sky Suite 1228 on the MV *Galaxy* using an online travel agency. My hand shook when it came time to hit the confirmation button.

I raced downstairs and made the announcement. "I did it."

Kris looked up from her latest book and said, "Did what?"

"I booked it."

"Booked what?"

"The anniversary cruise. Ten days on a western Caribbean itinerary, sailing from Baltimore to Key West, Cozumel, Belize, Coco Cay and Nassau."

"You're kidding, right?"

"No, I really did it."

"It doesn't stop in St. Thomas?"

"Not on this route. They do offer an 11-day trip that includes St. Thomas, but I thought ten days would be enough. We'll see a lot of new places."

"Are you sure we should do this? Ten days? Who's going to watch Wells?" asked Kris, referring to our 16-year-old son.

"Ryan," I answered. Our 23-year-old son had recently settled in Philadelphia, and I'd hatched an elaborate plan. "We'll drive to Philadelphia, and Ryan will drive us to the ship in Baltimore. Then he'll drive our car back to New Hampshire to stay here with Wells while we're gone."

"He's willing to do that?" asked Kris.

"He will be," I answered with confidence. "It'll be like a vacation for him. All expenses paid."

"You haven't asked him yet?"

"No...I'll call him right now." I phoned Ryan. His job was flexible enough to allow the time away, and he thought it was a great plan. "See," I said to Kris. "We're all set."

Once the trip was booked, we entered a whole new phase of planning. Over the next few days, Kris devoured all of the information I had collected about cruising. I, on the other hand, started to feel some buyer's remorse—especially when it became clear that buying the tickets was just the beginning. What had I done?

"We'll have to get a whole new wardrobe," said Kris.

"Why?" I wondered aloud.

"And luggage, too."

"Why?"

"Because we don't have any," Kris answered.

"Clothes?"

"No," Kris said with mock exasperation. "Luggage...and we really should get some new clothes. You are going to get a tuxedo, aren't you?"

"A tux? What for?"

"For the formal dinners."

For evening wear, the cruise had three distinct modes. Kris read aloud from a brochure: "On formal nights, both men and women may prefer more dressy attire, such as an evening gown for women and a tuxedo or dark suit for men. On informal nights, men are requested to wear a jacket, shirt and tie, while women may want to wear a suit or dress. A gentleman's choice for casual nights includes a sport shirt and slacks, while women will be comfortable in a suit, skirt and blouse, or a dress."

"It says you can just wear a dark suit. I haven't worn a tux since the senior prom."

"That's not true. You wore one when we got married."

"Oops…I forgot about that. So I haven't worn one in twenty-five years—I'm getting along just fine, thanks."

"But you'll look so handsome in a tux." Kris turned on the charm and activated her most coquettish expression. "Picture it—you and me in the casino—it'll be like we're in a James Bond movie. Please?"

"What character would I be? Oddjob?"

"Come on. It'll be fun," she said. For just a moment, I saw a genuine twinkle in her eye.

I wasn't about to fall for it. "My suit will be fine. It's only ten years old, and I've only worn it once."

"You're no fun. I can't believe you won't wear a tuxedo for me. Pretty please?"

"No," I said with finality. Kris pouted, but I kept my resolve.

Later that night, I was reading through the forum on CruiseCritic when I stumbled upon a discussion entitled "Tuxedo on Galaxy—Should I or Shouldn't I?" Here are some excerpts from the discussion:

> …I would just like to hear your thoughts on the issue…to tux or not to tux, that is the question? Hey, stupid question, but I've been reading suggestions on which ship to sail based on how the eggs benedict were prepared!!!

> …And if the sparkle in your wife's eyes when she sees others dressed formally isn't enough to motivate you, think of how that sparkle will really shine when she sees you all decked out…go for it…

> …How many times in her life does your wife get to dress in a gown and go out with a man in a tux? This means a *lot* to many women, me included. If my husband were the only man on board to wear a tux, I would still hope he would do that for me because it means a lot. That sparkle in her eye should be all the answer you need…

> …I was discussing this topic at work and the best response I got follows: If she loves him enough to stay married after seeing him sitting around in his boxers and T-shirt, drinking beer, eating chips and watching football…perhaps he'll love her enough to wear a tux, especially if just the thought of him dressing up puts a twinkle in her eye…

After reading a few of the messages, I turned to mush and had second thoughts about my position on the tux. For the first time, I was motivated to actually write something and post it on the discussion board. Here it is:

> Aw-shucks. Maybe I shouldn't have read this thread. I saw that exact twinkle in her eye when my wife asked if I planned to get a tux. I declined. She went

on, dreamily, about the romance and the James Bondishness of going to the champagne bar or the casino dressed to the nines. I stood my ground, seeking some way to economize on the otherwise lavish trip. Then, I read this thread. We are cruising to celebrate our twenty-fifth anniversary, and I just never imagined that a tux might play such a major role in enhancing the experience—at least for her. Now I know better. So, if you see a couple in the casino, she in a lavish gown decades out of date and he obviously ill-at-ease in a used but serviceable tux—neither looking anything remotely like characters from a James Bond movie—stop and say hello.

A few minutes later, I found the tuxedo rental Web site and reserved a penguin suit for the cruise. For a modest fee, the tuxedo would be delivered directly to our stateroom—one less thing to pack and carry. I decided that the tuxedo would be a surprise, so in further discussions on the topic I steadfastly refused to consider wearing one on the cruise. Kris was not pleased.

We spent many hours agonizing over the selection of shore excursions. Many people proudly book them on their own with independent operators, but we decided that sticking with the ship's offerings would make life simpler. Even so, the range of interesting destinations and activities made choosing difficult. After much discussion, we agreed on a set of excursions that took best advantage of each port's uniqueness.

"Do we need passports?" asked Kris.

"Technically, we don't need them," I answered. "A driver's license and birth certificate will do it."

"What if we get stranded somewhere?"

"The ship won't leave without us if we're on one of their tours," I said.

"Are you sure?" asked Kris.

"Absolutely."

"What about the places where we aren't doing an excursion—like Nassau?"

"It might not be so bad to get stuck on a tropical island," I answered. Later, I thought about the possibilities and had a change of heart. We got passports—couldn't hurt.

I refined the travel plans a bit. Celebrity offered bus transfer to the ship from suburban Philadelphia, which would save Ryan the trouble of driving us to Baltimore. I searched the Internet for hotels close to the pick-up point and found one that appeared to be within walking distance.

"Are you sure it's close?" asked Kris when I told her about the new plan.

I showed her the map that I printed from the Internet. "Look. Here's the bus stop," I said, pointing to a little red dot. "And here's the hotel."

"Remember what happened the last time we used a map from the Internet?"

I did. The map was just plain wrong, and we went around in circles looking for a place that was actually miles away. "What's the worst that can happen? We can always take a taxi."

"This sure is getting complicated," Kris said.

"What's the matter?" I asked.

"I don't know. On one hand, I'm really excited. But I guess I'm just worried that we're going to spend all this money on a trip and we aren't going to like it," she said.

"I know the feeling," I said. "It's like I'm preoccupied with thoughts of the cruise. I keep building up expectations until I realize that they're completely unrealistic and then I start thinking about what a dumb idea this is. I wish we could just go today and get it over with."

"Me, too," said Kris.

"It can't be that bad, I suppose. I read that nine million people from North America cruise every year. Can nine million people be wrong?" Kris gave me a sideways glance and held it. "What?" I asked. She raised an eyebrow. Finally, I said, "OK, I withdraw the question."

Packing for the cruise was a bit of a challenge. We found many sources on the Internet that provided helpful cruise packing lists. Using them for guidance, we made up our own. It ran about four printed pages. As the anticipation continued to build during the weeks before the cruise, we assembled everything on our list. This involved several trips to the mall wherein we each acquired what amounted to a new wardrobe. A trip to a discount store got us a new set of matching luggage. As the departure date approached, it seemed that every spare surface in the house sported a pile of cruise essentials. There was a toiletries pile, an underwear pile, a documents pile, a cosmetics pile, and piles for ultra casual wear, casual wear, informal wear, formal wear, shoes for all occasions, swimwear, electronics, daypacks, and random necessities. It seemed to me that we were buying and piling up things that we had managed to live without for decades, all for the sake of a 10-day vacation.

"This is getting ridiculous," I said to Kris. "We need to reconsider whether we need some of the things on the list. Do you really need cotton balls?"

"Yes, I do. Why do you need duct tape?"

"Because duct tape will fix anything. What if the strap on your bathing suit breaks?"

"I'll tie it," Kris said.

"What if you break your glasses?"

"I will not walk around with a wad of duct tape on my glasses. I refuse."

On the day before our departure, we methodically stuffed everything into the suitcases. Among the more useful packing tips I found was the suggestion to put items like socks, T-shirts and underwear into zip-lock bags. When filled, you can sit on them to compress the contents and squeeze out the air. When you zip them up, you end up with vacuum-packed BVDs. It really helps save space. As I sat on my bag of undies, I could feel the roll of duct tape digging in to my behind. I hid my grimace from Kris.

I asked for a little more help than was really necessary when packing my dark suit, hoping to prolong the tuxedo ruse for as long as possible.

"I read that if you put a big plastic bag over things like *dark suits for formal night* they won't get wrinkled in the garment bag." Kris patiently slipped a big black garbage bag over the suit while I held it aloft.

When we finished packing, we had two giant suitcases, two garment bags, a medium suitcase, an overnight bag, a fake leather briefcase full of documents, two daypacks, a nylon bag containing speakers for the portable stereo system, and Kris's pocketbook.

"Good thing we don't have to fly. They'd never let us on the plane with all this stuff," I said.

"How are we going to carry it all?"

I demonstrated how the new suitcases were designed to hook together into two bulky but manageable rolling fortresses. Onto each large suitcase, I strapped two more bags. That left the odd pieces to deal with individually, but with some bungee cords, I managed to hook them all on to the rolling bases.

"There," I said with satisfaction. I extended the handle of one of the large suitcases and pulled, but the assembly did not budge. I had to put my weight on it to get the thing to tip forward onto its wheels. The handle flexed ominously, but the contrivance did roll quite nicely. It didn't want to stop once underway, but you can't have everything.

Kris tried the other luggage unit. "This must weigh a hundred pounds," she said.

"Well, you're the one who needed to bring cotton balls. Don't blame me. Do we have everything?"

"I certainly hope so," Kris replied.

For a finishing touch, I slipped a sheet of paper with our full identification into each bag. I then secured each zipper with a cable tie—an ingenious device made for electrical wiring, but also handy for locking suitcases. I left the medium suitcase unsecured as it contained everything we'd need to survive until we were settled on the ship.

"How do you get those things off?" asked Kris, curious about the cable ties.

"You have to cut them. You'll know immediately if someone has been in your bag," I answered.

"How are you going to cut them?"

I was momentarily thrown for a loop. "With the fingernail clippers," I finally said.

"Where are they?"

"They're in the big…Don't worry; they'll have something on the ship that we can use. It'll work out."

On Thursday, July 18, we packed the car and made the long drive to Philadelphia. Using the Internet map, we drove around in circles looking for the hotel. Although we could see it, getting there was another matter. After checking in, I discovered that the bus stop was at a McDonald's restaurant directly across the street. Our window offered a grand view of it. We met Ryan for dinner, and he dropped us off afterward so he could take our car.

"Tomorrow's the day," I said to Kris as we prepared for bed.

"What time do we leave?"

"The bus will be here at 11:00 a.m., so we can sleep late," I said.

"I don't think I remember how to sleep late."

"Try it," I said. "You're on vacation now…"

To the Ship

Friday, July 19

We both slept late. It's like riding a bike—you never forget. I happened to be looking out the window of the hotel room at about 10:20 a.m. when I saw a bus pull into the McDonald's parking lot. We'd barely had time for coffee.

"It's here!" I exclaimed.

"The bus? But we're not ready! Isn't it supposed to be here at eleven o'clock?"

"Yeah, but that must be it." I was starting to doubt that it was actually our bus, but we finished packing the luggage in a panic and rushed from the hotel—just in case.

"Taxi, sir?" called a cab driver.

"No thanks," I replied without pausing. If he had said "To the ship?" we might have taken him up on the offer. The hotel's entry was not designed for pedestrians, and we had to run down the steeply sloping driveway dodging limousines and taxicabs.

We made it to the street without incident. Traffic whizzed by nonstop in both directions, and there was not a sidewalk, crosswalk, or traffic light within sight. Eventually a driver took pity on us and stopped. Others followed suit, probably to gawk at the spectacle of two people struggling with a huge load of luggage. We must have been quite a sight. We ran across the street to the bus, where our driver calmly greeted us.

"Are you going to the cruise ship?" he asked.

"Yup," I said. "Are you early?"

"We're *way* ahead of schedule. I thought we'd have to wait here for a while, but you are the last people we need to pick up. My name is Henry. Let's get you on board—we'll head out to Baltimore right away."

Henry stored our bags in the luggage compartment while we joined a group of expectant cruisers on the bus. There was plenty of room, so Kris and I each took a double seat. We immediately left for Baltimore, thirty minutes ahead of schedule.

The bus made a brief lunch stop at a rest area in Delaware. Most of the passengers went inside for something to eat, but it looked like a madhouse. Kris and I decided to remain outside.

A few minutes after we arrived, the bus sitting next to ours loaded up and backed out of its parking space. An elderly woman calmly walked up to our bus, ascended the stairs, and paused at the top. She turned and came back down the stairs, looked at me, looked at Kris, and finally, with puzzlement creeping over her face, she turned to Henry.

"This isn't my bus," the woman said. "Where's my bus?"

We all looked at the neighboring bus as it passed behind ours and headed for the entrance ramp. The elderly woman took off in a surprisingly sprightly sprint through the smoky wake of her bus. She waved her arms frantically as she ran, as though she was trying to catch up with the departing bus by flying. "Stop! Wait! Hey!" she yelled, to no avail.

Shouting a similar refrain, Henry tried to get the woman to stop. His efforts were no more successful than hers. The bus steadily receded into the distance, but the woman did not give up until she was about to merge onto Interstate 95 herself. Finally, she turned and began walking back in our direction.

"That's right, darlin'—come on back," said Henry. He retrieved his cell phone from the bus and used it to call his dispatcher, describing the situation. He was able to provide the name of the bus line that had left the woman behind.

When the woman finally made it back to our bus, Henry asked her where they were headed.

"We're going to Williamsburg," she answered. "What am I going to do? I can't believe they left me."

"Don't you worry, darlin'. We're gonna take care of everything," Henry replied. "You just get y'self on this bus and get cooled off."

Henry relayed the additional information to the dispatcher, who ultimately got word to the woman's bus. By now, the passengers on our bus had returned and were in on the drama. Henry made a careful count before departing and declared, "Good, we've got one too many. Let's go!"

Bus travel isn't usually the most pleasant form of transportation, but with the combination of our destination and this extra little adventure, the mood on board was practically giddy. Many miles down the highway, we pulled off to the side of the road behind the wayward bus. As our stowaway prepared to rejoin her tour, the passengers broke into a spontaneous chorus of "For He's a Jolly Good Fellow." Henry helped the women off the bus, where her driver waited with apologies.

After a harrowing merge back onto I-95 from the breakdown lane, we passed a miles-long northbound traffic jam. I hoped we weren't witnessing the usual condition for this roadway, because our return trip would be miserable. Our southbound trip continued without any traffic problems. Before long, the bus exited the interstate and entered an industrial area.

Henry got on the PA system and made an announcement. "Ladies and gentlemen, as soon as we pass this building you'll be able to see the ship…there she is. Isn't she a beauty?" I caught fleeting glimpses of *Galaxy* as we navigated through the streets. She was an impressive sight, dwarfing everything nearby. The day was murky, but somehow the ship gleamed as if spotlighted. A few minutes later, at 1:15 p.m., Henry dropped us about fifty feet from the entrance to the cruise terminal. The building appeared to be a hastily converted warehouse, and it blocked most of the ship's superstructure from view.

As we climbed down the steps from the bus and into the oppressive heat of the day, Henry chanted: "Thank you…watch your step…take your carry-on baggage and leave the big stuff with me. It'll be delivered to your cabin…see you next week. Have a great trip!"

Entering the terminal, the check-in lines were on our right. From my reading, I was prepared to stand in one long line after another in a lengthy and complex check-in and boarding process. Indeed, many dozens stood in line waiting for their turn to see a check-in agent. To our left, a large seating area was filled with people. They were apparently waiting to be called to join a line snaking through a roped area leading to the gangway.

I spotted a sign indicating a line specifically for suite passengers. To my surprise, there was no one at all in this line and we made our way without delay to the check-in counter. I presented our ticket book to a smiling woman in a blue uniform.

The woman typed something into a computer. "I see we already have all of your information. Very good." I had submitted our personal data through a convenient Internet form, so we avoided the need to fill out a paper immigration questionnaire.

"May I have your credit card, please?" asked the woman "It will be used to cover your on-board expenses."

I handed the card over, and the woman made an imprint before handing it back. In response to a few keystrokes, a nearby machine produced two gold-colored plastic cards.

"These cards are used for all charges on the ship, and they are also your room keys. Welcome to *Galaxy*, Mr. and Mrs. 'X.' You can proceed to the waiting area…"

A young woman who had been standing silently in the background suddenly sprang forward. "Thank you. I'll be taking care of Mr. and Mrs. 'X.' Will you come with me, please?" She unhooked a rope barrier and invited us to join her behind the check-in counter. *Great*, I thought. *We're already in trouble.* I prepared for some kind of bad news. *Is there a problem back home? Are they putting us in steerage?*

"I'm so glad to see you, Mr. And Mrs. 'X.' I'm Liz…" She gave us her title, but I was so concerned about what was coming that it didn't register. "Is this your first time sailing with Celebrity?"

"First cruise, period," answered Kris.

I couldn't bear it any longer. "Is there a problem?" I asked, confident that I already knew the answer. *All that planning and preparation—good thing we bought the travel insurance.* I could feel a bead of nervous sweat building on my brow.

"Oh no, not at all," Liz said with a laugh. "I just want to welcome you on behalf of Celebrity Cruises."

We continued to chat for a few minutes. Liz asked all sorts of questions about us and our plans, seeming like a long-absent friend catching up on the news. Finally at ease, I mentioned the fact that we were cruising in honor of our twenty-fifth anniversary.

"Oh, what a wonderful way to celebrate. You are going to have a super trip! Let's get a picture of you two."

Liz escorted us across a section of the room shielded by curtains from the public area. Along the way, she summoned a tuxedoed butler, who took our carry-on baggage with white-gloved hands. Reaching the far side of the curtained area, Liz poked her head through an opening and spoke to someone. A moment later, she directed us to slip through the curtain. On the other side, we found ourselves at a brightly lit photographer's station. While dozens of people waited patiently in line, we posed for a couple of quick shots in front of a welcome aboard prop. When we rejoined Liz and the heavily laden butler behind the curtain, an armed security guard had joined the party. At the sight of him, the sliver of lingering anxiety reconstituted. *So there is a problem…*

"Are you ready?" asked Liz.

"Sure. Let's give it a try," I answered.

"Bon Voyage!" she exclaimed, indicating with a wave that we should follow the guard. "See you later."

The guard led us through another opening in the curtain. This time, we emerged on the business side of a baggage-screening machine. Another long line of people waited to pass through the security checkpoint, but the guard held up his hands like a traffic cop to allow the butler to place our bags on the conveyor. Kris and I were escorted through a metal detector. The guard departed, leaving us to wait for the butler to catch up.

My expectations for the trip were already greatly exceeded, but I was feeling more than a little guilty and mystified about the special treatment.

"All those people waiting in line must hate us," I said to Kris. "This is really strange."

"The cruise people must think we're someone else."

"Well, I'm not going to complain."

The butler arrived, and we paused for a brief introduction. He was a young gentleman from Bombay, relatively new in his role. We followed him onto the covered gangway where a rush of cold air made me realize just how hot and sultry the day had become. At the top of the gangway, we entered the ship just aft of the guest relations desk in the Grand Foyer on deck five. We were instructed to insert our plastic cards into a slot and peer down at a camera in the security podium for a picture. From then on when we inserted our cards upon entering the ship, our photos would flash onto a screen in front of the security guard.

The butler led us through the throng of people who were entering and being met by white-gloved escorts. We took the mirrored elevator to deck twelve and rounded a corner to enter a long corridor lined with rich woods and shiny brass accents. Partway down the corridor, we stopped at a door marked 1228. The butler opened the door with one of our cards, deposited our bags on the bed, and departed. "Good day, sir. Good day, madam."

It was not yet 1:30 p.m., a scant fifteen minutes since we stepped off the bus. I hadn't even had time to take my camera out of the bag for a couple of pictures.

I looked at Kris and opened my mouth, not sure what to say. "Wow!" is what eventually came out.

Onboard Galaxy

Friday, July 19

We did a quick survey of the room. Sky Suite 1228 is on the starboard side of the ship, about fifty feet forward of the aft elevator tower. It is slightly smaller than your average hotel room but is well designed, stylish, and very comfortable. Two people can maneuver about with little interference (we heard this was not the case in smaller accommodations). Rather than bore you with the extreme details now, a complete description of the cabin is available on my Web site (book.chestcrh.com). Read it if you like, at your leisure.

Goodies of various sorts were placed throughout the cabin—a bottle of champagne on ice, fresh flowers, a tray of hors d'oeuvres, and a fruit basket.

"Is this caviar?" I asked, holding up one of the hors d'oeuvres.

Kris looked it over. "Sure is." She's so much more sophisticated than I am.

"Should we toast?"

"Why not? We're on vacation," Kris answered.

I plucked the champagne from the ice bucket. "I'd better pop the cork outside, just in case. Open the curtains so I can go out on the verandah."

Kris pulled the curtains aside and opened the door. We stepped out and were both immediately impressed by the size of the verandah.

"This is huge!" said Kris. The table for four and two lounge chairs didn't occupy more than a quarter of the space.

"Oh yeah...this is gonna be fine." I approached the chest-high railing and looked cautiously over the edge. We were at least eighty feet above the dock, and I felt a touch of vertigo.

I stepped back from the edge and regained my equilibrium. The cork didn't give me any trouble, and we made our toast. "Happy anniversary," I offered.

"Happy anniversary, dear. Here's to a good time."

"Let's hope," I said. "Let's hope..."

Sipping champagne, we watched the ship's restocking operation from the verandah. Truckload upon truckload of supplies arrived at the dock. Pallets were offloaded and placed on the ground, where a guard and a dog carefully examined each one. I don't know if they were looking for drugs or bombs, or both. After inspection, pallets were marked and then loaded directly onto deck three of the ship. Each dog worked for about fifteen minutes and then had a play break as another dog was pressed into service—they seemed to be having a great time. Access to the dock and ship were heavily guarded, and a police boat continually circled in the harbor.

"I'm getting awfully warm out here," I said to Kris. "Let's go take a look around."

We set off to explore the ship. Despite hours of pouring over deck plans and photographs, we still found ourselves in a strange land. The ship is much more massive than any image I had formed in my head—it seemed to go on forever in all directions. Partway through our tour, I regretted not bringing the map provided in the cabin's literature rack.

Resolving to use the stairs to burn off calories, we descended to deck four for a look at the medical center—this would come in handy later. It was surprisingly large and appeared well equipped. Climbing back up to deck five, we took a look at the guest relations and shore excursions desks as new passengers continued to stream in. At the guest relations desk, various cookbooks by Michel Roux were displayed and offered for sale. Roux is recognized as one of the world's most accomplished French chefs. As Celebrity's culinary and wine consultant, he creates the line's menus and wine lists, and oversees training of the restaurant staff.

"Look—a book just on sauces," said Kris. "Haven't you been looking for one of these?"

"Sure have." I picked up a copy and perused it.

"Do you want to get it?" Kris asked.

"It won't work," I said.

"Why not?" asked Kris.

"Everything is in metric. Remember when Tone made bread for us?"

Kris smiled and nodded. "I see your point," she said.

Many years ago, we employed a wonderful Norwegian au pair named Tone (pronounced, roughly, as "tuna"). She truly became a member of the family. When I got home from work one day, Tone told me that the oven wasn't working correctly. As a surprise, she made some Norwegian bread to accompany dinner. It had been in the oven for more than five hours. "It still isn't cooked," she told me.

I went to investigate, and found the problem immediately. "The oven is set to 200 degrees," I said.

"I called my mother. She said that was the right temperature," Tone replied.

I broke the news to her. "We're not like the rest of the world. This oven works in Fahrenheit, not Celsius." I fetched my calculator, and punched in some digits. "It needs to be set at about 400 degrees." Tone adjusted the oven, but it was far too late. The loaf would have made an effective doorstop.

"I don't want to keep a calculator in the kitchen," I said, placing the book back on the shelf. "Too bad."

On an easel opposite the excursion desk, a large map detailed our planned route. We were going to cover a lot of ground—make that a lot of water—on this trip, and the map displayed interesting details about our exact route. I stood and examined it until Kris dragged me away.

A massive staircase rising through four decks defines the Grand Foyer. Behind the staircase is a giant three-story painting of a Victorian girl on a swing, which we studied intently as we climbed up to take in the public areas on decks six and seven.

All the way forward, nestled into the bow of the ship and spanning two decks, we found the Celebrity Theater. Seating 904 people, the theater has some features that you'll wish for in your local venue. There are lighted tables for drinks spaced so that patrons are seated a very comfortable distance apart. The couch-like seating has headrests, ideal for those prone to dozing during performances. The aisles are so wide that no one has to stand to allow other patrons into or out of the interior seating positions. Waiter service is featured during performances. Sight lines are quite good, although in the balconies you may have to crane a bit to see the front part of the stage. The lighting and audio equipment are first rate. Overall, the theater is a fantastic place to see a show.

There are a number of shops, including a liquor store (very good prices), and a little general store for expensive sundries (aspirin, Tylenol, seasickness and cold remedies, candies, paperbacks, film, and cigarettes by the carton). The Logo Shop offers T-shirts, polo shirts, men's bathing suits, coffee cups and mugs, jackets, knickknacks, notepads, photo albums, kid's toys, and stuffed animals—almost everything sporting a Celebrity logo. A perfume shop contains smelly stuff, a jewelry shop has sparkly stuff, and an upscale clothing store also dispenses costume jewelry. Adjacent to the shops is a long, narrow video game arcade. I made a mental note to check it out in detail, but never got to it. I stuck with the games that take and dispense quarters in more prodigious quantities.

There is a game room and an open area containing a few Internet stations just outside the Celebrity Theater entrance. I just peeked in to the movie theater and never realized my ambition to try the ship's popcorn. Several films were shown during the cruise, but the schedules just didn't work for us.

On the first day, the Internet stations were posted at fifty cents a minute. After that, the sale signs disappeared and the charge went back to the regular $1 per minute. Figure on $4–$5 to check for an e-mail from the kids and to send one to them—even though they didn't write to you. You'll need to use one of the Internet-based e-mail services, such as yahoo.com. If you don't already have an account, get one beforehand and save the $10 it would cost to use the ship's Internet connection for sign-up.

Seating areas are scattered everywhere. Many are convenient to one bar or another, but there are plenty of quiet nooks great for reading. The Cova Café di Milano, a coffee and pastry bar featuring international coffees, is particularly attractive and uncrowded. In the case of Rendezvous Square, the concepts of bar, lounge, seating area, and main hallway all merge into one. In fact, the casino, the art gallery, photo display and sales area are all an integral part of the public passageways—for all practical purposes, unavoidable.

From deck six, there are several doors allowing access to an exterior promenade situated under the lifeboats. The promenade has a nice teak deck, which is marked for shuffleboard. All of the metal is painted dark blue, highlighted by brass fixtures. Forward, the promenade ends in a tunnel alongside the theater. Aft, it rises to deck seven where you can walk all the way around the stern, down the steps, and back along the opposite side of the ship. To me, this overlooked area exudes the most ship-like feeling to be found anywhere on board—you can see and hear the bow wake and smell the water. From the higher decks, the relationship with the sea is not nearly so intimate.

The Orion Restaurant spans two decks, with a sweeping central staircase connecting the levels. Upper and lower entrances are on decks six and five respectively. Windows surround the room on three sides, with a set of curved windows soaring two levels behind the captain's table in the open central section at the stern. From the outside, the dining room windows and the curved bump-out comprise the best looking part of the ship—reminiscent of an old Spanish galleon. Simply stated, *Galaxy* has a nice butt.

Close to 1,000 people dine in the Orion Restaurant each night at 6:00 p.m. and again at 8:30. There is one ladies' room outside the lower level, and it is utterly and completely inadequate for the crowd that emerges after each dinner seating. The only alternative is to walk all the way forward to the theater area, but you will burn some calories and save some time and aggravation by doing so. In addition, you'll be right there ready to see the show.

Casino Royale is a big flashy noisy place in what is otherwise an understated and soothing ship. Nevertheless, it manages to seem cave-like and intimate. I remember reading that there are over 250 slot machines. I didn't pay close attention, but I saw one roulette wheel, one craps table, a few blackjack tables, and a couple of poker tables.

"I want to try blackjack," said Kris. Aside from nickel poker at the family camp in Maine and a lifelong losing streak on the occasional lottery ticket, neither of us had ever gambled.

I surveyed a blackjack table. "Minimum bet is $5. Maximum, $100," I read from a sign posted nearby.

"Five dollars! That's way too much!"

"The slots are all nickel and quarter machines. Maybe we should just try those," I said.

"Good idea."

"How 'bout this," I said. "We'll allocate $20 a night to the casino, and see what happens." If she wanted James Bond, by gosh...

"I can go for that. Twenty dollars, and no more." Kris would make a good Miss Moneypenny.

Aft of the casino is an art gallery. Running the width of the ship, it displays artwork to be sold at the frequent auctions (a ubiquitous cruise ship activity). There were a few interesting pieces now and then (cartoon cels, for example), but we never made it to an auction. We don't have any more hanging space at home.

The photography area on deck six is used to display the thousands of pictures taken and printed by the ship's photographers. From embarkation to the last day, photo opportunities abound. Shortly after embarkation, the welcome aboard photos taken in the terminal building are displayed. Small photos (5 by 7 inches) go for about $10. On formal nights, there are various photo stations set up for posed shots. Both the picture size and price go up. Suite passengers get a complimentary private sitting, which means you don't have to stand in line with everyone else on formal night. However, you will pay $25 for each copy of any of the three poses taken. Inquire at the photo sales desk. You are under no obligation to purchase anything, but you probably will. Price breaks, frames, ship pictures, and other extras are offered as incentives to buy photos in quantity.

The library and computer room are on deck eight, marking the top of the four-level Grand Foyer. On the ceiling between them is a giant working compass, best viewed from several decks below. The library is small, but if you've forgotten to bring a book, you can probably find something. The computers here are the same as are found in several other places. With a swipe of your cashless cruising card, you're in. In addition to Internet access, common business applications

(Word, Excel, etc.) are available. Each cluster of computers has an attached laser printer.

Decks eight through ten are the primary hotel decks. Standing at one end of the ship and looking down the 800-foot corridors is disorienting. The sensation is like being in a house of mirrors, with duplicate images marching off into infinity. Deck nine holds the Ship Mates Fun Factory, which looks like a well-equipped day-care center. A wading pool with a cute serpent slide sits outside on the stern, sheltered by the deck above.

Deck eleven features a very nice outdoor café at the stern. Lots of tables with umbrellas make this a great place to sit and watch the wake of the ship. Snacks and drinks are often available at the adjacent Oasis Pool, situated under a massive sliding roof. The Oasis is a beautiful spot where you can lounge poolside among large tropical plants in air-conditioned comfort. The interior area around this pool is used for the alternative evening dining option. Reservations are required, and a $2 gratuity is requested.

Moving forward, we entered the Oasis Café, which hosts breakfast and lunch buffets in addition to an evening sushi bar. Lunch was being served, so we decided to partake. There are four identical serving lines in the central area, with seating around the outside in a series of large-windowed bays that cantilever from the side of the ship. On top of these bays sit the sky suite verandahs.

A waiter approached Kris with a tray of exotic tropical drinks. She was an easy mark, especially when told that she could keep the tall frosted glass decorated with exotic flowers and drink recipes. I signed the charge slip for $8.50 and suggested she ask for a plastic cup next time. As it turned out, this was the closest thing to hawking drinks that we experienced onboard *Galaxy*.

I filled a plate with all kinds of goodies including fish, chicken, freshly carved roast beef, and a sampler of six or seven different kinds of salad. I filled another plate with desserts. As soon as we turned around, waiters stepped up to carry our food to an empty table. We ate heartily, and I got myself one of those fancy drinks so that Kris's souvenir glass wouldn't get lonely.

Exiting the Oasis Café, we moved forward to the Ocean Pool. This was still in surprising disarray from the previous cruise, but it was early and most passengers were still on shore. We moved forward in search of the spa to book our major anniversary gift, an in-suite massage. A professional massage would be another first for both of us. Over the years, we have tried to comfort each other with a massage method that usually elicits more ticklish laughter than relaxation. Entering the forward superstructure on the starboard side, we found locked doors where memory said the spa should be located—so we popped up one flight to check out the Stratosphere Lounge.

The Stratosphere, with its 14-foot floor-to-ceiling wraparound windows, provides a stunning view. The huge room contains several levels of seating surrounding a big dance floor. One of the Stratosphere's bars has a big-screen TV, usually tuned to sporting events. Sports bars are the latest fad in cruise ship design, so this must be *Galaxy's* attempt to retrofit the concept. A quick peek into the teen disco revealed a small space that we were bound never to enter.

"Well, that's the end of our tour," I said to Kris. "What do you think?"

"Amazing. I can't believe how big it is."

"We only saw about half of the ship," I said. "We'll see the rest later. Let's go back to the cabin and get settled."

Back outside on deck twelve, we walked aft around the upper pool lounge area and into the structure containing the sky suites. In our cabin, three of four pieces of checked luggage had arrived and Raj, the butler, was waiting. It was only 3:30 p.m.

The Disaster, the Drill, the Departure, and the Dinner

Friday, July 19

Raj introduced himself and helped us settle into the room with some cappuccino and more hors d'oeuvres. Hailing from Goa, India, Raj is tall and thin and a perfect gentleman. He introduced the stateroom attendants, Muriel and Reynaldo, who were exceedingly pleasant. We delayed unpacking and hung out on the verandah to watch the activity as supplies and passengers continued to arrive. We later learned that for the 10-day sailing, 800,000 pounds of provisions are loaded.

I took some time to read through the binder of information on the desk. In the daily activity newsletter, I found an article on the spa and its services.

"We'd better go find the spa," I said to Kris. "It says here that some services sell out quickly."

"It was closed. Remember?"

"I don't think we were in the right place. It's supposed to be open all day."

We headed back out in search of the spa entrance to book the massages. Shortly after 4:30 p.m., we found the correct door on the port side, and got in a long line of people with similar intentions. The line hardly seemed to move. It stretched around a corner, so we couldn't even tell how far we were from the reservation desk.

I kept looking at my watch. The mandatory lifeboat drill was scheduled for 5:15 p.m., now only twenty-five minutes away. The spa manager walked down the line advising people that they might not make it to the service desk before then.

"This doesn't look good," I said. "That's a shame."

"A massage was the one thing I was really looking forward to," said Kris. "Let's just go back to the room."

"Maybe you're right. I can give you a massage instead."

Kris didn't answer, but she made no move to leave, either. When I looked around, the few people who were in line behind us had vanished. As the minutes passed, people in front of us also gave up and left. Perhaps they were all better than we were at giving spousal massages.

Our persistence paid off. With two minutes to go, we arrived at the desk and requested a couple's massage. Information about the sky suite indicated that en suite massages were available, so that is what I asked for.

The woman at the desk was puzzled by my request. "A massage on your verandah, sir? I'm not sure if we can do that." She called the spa manager over for consultation. In short order, our request was granted and a reservation for the following afternoon was on the books. As we turned from the desk, the PA system came to life. An announcement instructed everyone to get their life jackets and report to their assigned muster stations.

We hurriedly walked aft toward the pool deck and our cabin beyond.

"See, patience is a virtue," I said, turning to Kris. "I can't believe how well this trip is…"

Wham! I was stunned by a collision with an automatic sliding glass door that was in much less of a hurry than I was. I did not see it at all. Certainly my eyesight has worsened with age, but I think maybe the glass was just too darned clean. My motto is: *A little dirt can prevent a hurt.*

"Ouch! Are you all right?" asked Kris. Actually, I don't know what she said, because the ringing in my ears was too loud. Stars swam before my eyes. "You're bleeding!"

I raised my hands to my head in an effort to keep it from exploding. Under my left hand, I could feel a sticky wetness. Seconds later, blood began dripping off my nose.

"I don't have any tissue. Come on, let's get you to the cabin," said Kris.

That sounded like a good idea. When I took a step, my leg buckled. "I hit my knee, too," I said.

"Can you walk?"

"I think so," I answered, overoptimistically.

The muster signal chimed repeatedly over the PA system as we continued toward the cabin. Muriel, the cabin attendant, spotted me limping down the corridor, dripping blood. She acquired the look of a concerned mother. After helping Kris get the cabin door open, Muriel got me a wad of Kleenex from the bathroom. Kris retrieved the life jackets from the closet, and I struggled to put mine on while keeping the tissue firmly planted against my forehead wound. We left the cabin and headed for the stairs.

"Come on. We have to hurry," said Kris.

"I'm doing my best."

During the drill, use of the elevators was restricted to handicapped passengers. I probably would have qualified for a temporary permit, but Kris ran and I limped down six flights of stairs to our assigned muster station in the casino. I think I was temporarily cross-eyed, and couldn't quite focus on anything. I felt and, I'm sure, looked like a complete idiot. A whopping headache set in. I was dizzy, which made it very difficult to stand on my remaining good leg—I couldn't put any weight on the injured one. I just wanted to lie down.

My main memory of the muster drill is fighting to remain upright while lined up six deep on the promenade under the lifeboats, shoulder to shoulder with 2000 other people, in the suffocating heat. The instructional narrative piped over the PA system concluded with a directive for people to keep their life jackets on and return to their cabins. Of course, half the people immediately began removing the jackets, and elbows, jackets, and other things were flying through the air perilously close to my aching head. At least the bleeding had slowed.

The climb back up the stairs was excruciating. What was really bugging me, though, was the announcer's voice. It was so familiar. I knew it from the movies or TV—a voice over narrator or something. Try as I might, I could not place it.

Back at the ranch, Muriel doted over me and suggested a visit to the medical center. Kris summoned her nursing skills and gave me a quick examination.

"It's a pretty good cut, right above your eyebrow. It's kind of a funny shape. You might need stitches," Kris said. "At least you should get it cleaned out." She agreed that a trip to the infirmary was advisable. "Do you want me to go with you?"

"No, that's all right," I replied. "Maybe you can work on unpacking while I'm gone. I don't want to miss the sail-away."

"How am I supposed to get the suitcases open?" asked Kris.

I looked around for something sharp to cut the intact cable ties, and found nothing better that a butter knife. Muriel stepped in and offered to help. "I will get some scissors, madam. Don't worry about it, sir—you go now!" she said. I knew it would all work out...

Before leaving for the infirmary, I swallowed a few Ibuprofen tablets with a champagne chaser. Hobbling to the elevator, I felt like a lame plow horse headed to the glue factory—convinced that the vacation-from-hell was just now beginning. It had all been going so well, but it was too late to turn back now.

The medical center already had a couple of clients, though no one else seemed to be bleeding. After a 5-minute wait, a nurse took me into an examining room. She spoke with a delightful British accent.

"Right then, let's have a look." She aimed a light at my face and wiped my brow. "Oh, that's lovely. Get into some fisticuffs over a lady, did you?"

"A door attacked me."

"One of the sliding ones?" She didn't seem surprised when I nodded. She cleaned out my wound and pronounced it unworthy of stitches. I expressed concern that I would scare my tablemates at the approaching dinner, so she made me a discreet bandage. The whole episode was handled with dispatch and good humor.

Dignity semi-preserved, I took the elevator back to the room. Muriel seemed relieved to see me in one piece. The final piece of luggage had arrived, and I helped Kris finish unpacking. I discreetly examined all of the closets for evidence of the tuxedo. Nothing. At least the surprise was still intact.

It was time for sail-away, right on schedule. A racket outside drew us to the verandah. A news helicopter hovered at eye-level a few hundred feet away, apparently dispatched to broadcast our departure between traffic reports. I retrieved my trusty video camera and began playing documentarian, taping the helicopter as it flew in circles around the ship.

We made our way forward and up some stairs leading to an open deck on top of the Stratosphere Lounge, the highest publicly accessible point on the ship. *Galaxy* cast off from the pier, moving almost imperceptibly through a 180-degree turn before heading out of the harbor toward Chesapeake Bay. Several boats accompanied us at a distance, and a few young men on jet skis showed less than good judgment as they crossed in front of *Galaxy*. She is a safe ship, but her brakes aren't so hot.

The ship passed under a series of bridges while exiting the harbor. I've driven across those bridges, and always wondered why they were built so ridiculously high. The answer became clear as the stack of the ship passed underneath them with only a few feet of clearance. It was a spectacular sight.

We finished off the champagne while watching the world go by from the verandah. There was remarkably little sense of motion, but we were still in sheltered waters. Soon enough it was time to get ready for dinner. Since it was a casual night, this was relatively easy—I just had to spruce up my bandage a bit. I put a single $20 bill in my pocket—the daily casino allocation.

We made our way to the Orion Restaurant clutching the card from our room that gave us claim to a spot at table 524. I had requested the late seating, which for us meant eating early. I do all the cooking at home. Arriving home around 7:00 p.m. on weekdays, I make a drink, read a newspaper or two, and then entertain the starving family with some kitchen antics—all this to avoid having to wash dishes.

I had requested a table for eight on the premise that there was bound to be someone compatible in such a large group. Table 524 was set for six, so our chances seemed considerably reduced.

Our tablemates turned out to be great company. Alan and Jodie came from Pennsylvania, while Mike and Jane lived in Virginia. Unlike us, they were all experienced cruisers. We all have similar numbers of dogs and children (very similar creatures from a caregiver's perspective), so there was plenty to talk about.

Our waiter, Bandasak, and his assistant, Joe, came from Thailand. I assume Joe was not a given name, but was more for our convenience. As we discovered, people from the same country are often assigned to work together so that they can communicate in their native language. Both Bandasak and Joe spoke English very well, and put everyone at ease with friendly banter.

And so, we ate. What a pleasurable experience. Kris had hake with cold pear and honey soup, finishing off with some freshly made rum-raisin ice cream. I had prime rib, medium rare on the nose, an oriental soup, a chocolate mousse toffee cake, and ice cream. Asking for multiple deserts became a ritual at our table.

My memories of this dinner are otherwise indistinct—my eyes were still crossed from the door episode. However, what I thought was just my head throbbing was later revealed to be a very loud and persistent low frequency noise coming from the propulsion systems below. It had a rhythm like a rail car over track joints at speed. This did not become clear until the second night.

After dinner, we made our way forward to the theater for the introductory show. It consisted of a lot of promotional talk and promises of things to come. There was that voice again, this time attached to an actual person—I still couldn't place it. As I've mentioned, the theater is very nice. I could stretch out my sore leg and rest my throbbing head, and the waiter was pleased to bring me an anesthetizing drink and set it on my table. It was refreshing to hear live musical accompaniment, which is becoming rare in many land-based theaters. The orchestra was the highlight of this show and they proved to be quite good.

"How do you feel?" asked Kris after the show.

"Like I have to go to bed," I said. "Immediately." This was not the night to get our casino initiation.

"Poor baby," she cooed. "Can I kiss it and make it better?"

"Maybe tomorrow," I answered.

In the cabin, I put the $20 bill back in the safe. I desperately wanted to sleep and see if my fears about a decline in vacation luck might evaporate with the dawn.

A Day at Sea

Saturday, July 20

I slept fitfully on the first night. I am normally a light sleeper, and the combination of pain, new sounds, and the ship's motions kept my mind in overdrive. We were in moderate seas, according to the weather report. The ship gently rocked from side to side in slow motion. In our bed, the motion meant that my feet and head were competing for the higher elevation. Underlying this motion were some very small and quick movements, like you feel in a train or plane. I can't imagine that a ship of such size could move as a whole at that frequency, so it must be flex within the structure itself. The cabin produced its own unique set of occasional creaks and groans.

At one point, I woke up and thought there was a duck in the room. Above the gentle whoosh of the air-conditioning, I heard a distinct "quack" every minute or so. I was ultimately driven to get up and find the source. I turned on the bathroom light and let it spill gently into the cabin, then stood perfectly still, listening. With each "quack," I fine-tuned my position until I finally honed in on the source—the minute hand advancing on the wall clock. It took until the third night for my body and brain to normalize all of these new sensations, after which I slept like a rock and needed a wake-up call to avoid sleeping until noon. Kris never lost a wink, except for this first morning when three or four slamming sounds would repeat every forty-five seconds or so—exactly long enough so that sleep was just returning when the sounds recurred. Finally fully awake, I realized that a jogger ignored the signs prohibiting use of the deck above us for a morning workout. It was 6:00 a.m.

"Should I call guest relations?" I whispered.

Kris mumbled something and turned on her side as the slamming sound passed overhead again. The phone was on her side of the bed, and I tried to summon the will to get up and use it. After four or five passes, the sound stopped. Someone else must have called. On subsequent days, the deck above our cabin was roped off and lounge chairs were wedged into the staircases to keep people away.

We slept until almost 9:00 a.m. Kris got first dibs on the shower, and was raring to go before I got out of bed. My head and knee were still throbbing with pain, and I must have looked ghastly.

"You need coffee," she said. "Should I call for some?"

"Here, this will be quicker." I limped over to the closet area where I retrieved two large insulated mugs from a drawer. In my quest to pack efficiently, I had stuffed the mugs with socks.

"I hope those socks were clean," said Kris.

"They're brand new—never worn." To be safe, I rinsed the mugs. "If you're willing, you can take these down to the café and fill them."

"What a great idea," said Kris. I couldn't take credit, though. The suggestion to bring mugs came from one of the online packing lists. It proved to be one of the most useful tips. The ship's coffee cups hold about one and a half swallows.

Kris popped down to the Oasis Café to fill the mugs with coffee, which is available there twenty-four hours a day. By the time I was clean and dressed, she was comfortably settled on the verandah. I joined her there, and we sipped coffee and took in the sweeping view of open ocean. It was very windy and already quite hot. I had never been out of sight of land on a boat of any kind, but quickly became comfortable with the idea. It was simply beautiful.

We seemed to be running in a defined shipping lane, as an occasional large freighter would pass on the port side. I could imagine a double yellow line separating us. Otherwise, nothing interrupted the horizon. The sea far below was covered with whitecaps, and the ship continued its gentle rocking.

One of our greatest concerns in preparing for the cruise was seasickness. Many people reported that the seas are often rough off the Carolinas, so in theory, this segment of the cruise would test our susceptibility. Our doctor prescribed scopolamine transdermal patches, an effective but somewhat controversial remedy. Many people suggested ginger capsules, which we found at a health food store and began using before we boarded the ship.

"So, is the motion bothering you?" I asked Kris.

"No, not at all. I like it. You?"

"No problem. I think I'm going to tempt fate and skip the ginger," I said.

"Are you sure? I'm going to keep taking it. I don't want any surprises," Kris said.

"Ready to eat?" I asked.

"Sure. Let's go."

I waited while Kris swallowed her dose of ginger—it was, in fact, the last she'd take—and then we headed to the Oasis where we had custom-built omelets. I took it as a good sign that the food went down easily and stayed there.

"What next?" I asked.

"I think some time in the thalassotherapy pool will make you feel better." We went back to the cabin and changed into swimwear before heading off to the spa. On the way, I approached the sliding glass door with caution. It opened quickly, and I passed through without incident.

Ah, the thalassotherapy pool—now here is a great invention. Complimentary to suite passengers (a daily use fee applies to others), it is a giant hyperactive hot tub with swirling, shooting, bubbling, pouring waters designed to massage different parts of the body as you move about. There is even a huge lounge chair, big enough for five people, underlain by powerful water jets. The cruise brochure advised that bathing suit fabrics might fade, and by the end of the cruise the suit I designated for use in the thalassotherapy pool had turned from dark to light. Be forewarned.

In the room containing the pool, there is also a steam room. It was incredibly hot—dangerously so, I thought. I could not stay in it more than a minute or two. When asked, the attendants said that they had been trying to get it fixed, but the solution continued to evade the technicians. Apparently, they remained stumped throughout the cruise.

Visible through glass facing forward, the gym was well stocked with exercise equipment, which was in constant use. People using the treadmills could look out over the bow of the ship, which must have produced the sensation of walking on water.

In the changing rooms there are lockers secured by a key obtained at the spa reception desk, which is also the source for towels. In addition to showers, the men's and women's changing rooms each contain a very nice sauna.

The thalassotherapy pool runs in cycles—about twenty-five minutes on and five minutes off. If you arrive and find calm water sloshing around, just get in and wait. Hang on to something though—the water jets are very powerful. After two cycles in the pool, we emerged, hit the sauna, showered, and emerged into daylight on the pool deck. I felt like a new person.

It was close enough to noon for a pina colada at the pool bar. The wind continued to blow at high strength, and it was difficult to walk a straight line on the exposed decks. The sun was shining brightly. Despite the wind, it was very hot—no surprise I suppose for July 20. Nevertheless, the pool area was full of happy people taking the whole thing in stride. I began to assume that this was a normal wind condition on a ship traveling on open water. This proved to be incorrect, as subsequent days were nothing more than pleasantly breezy.

When we went back to the room, things got really interesting. I was a minute behind Kris, having stopped to take some pictures. When I entered, she was hunched over—reading a folded card.

"Houston, we have a problem," she said. Her expression indicated shock and dismay.

"Oh, great—just when things were getting back on track. What is it?"

Kris didn't answer right away. I picked up the envelope that the card came in. In elegant script, it was addressed to:

Mr. And Mrs. "X"

Sky Suite 1228

At least bad news was delivered with style. I considered the possibilities for a moment. During our preparations, I'd mentioned the fact that passengers were sometimes invited to dine with the captain. I don't think Kris believed me at the time, and she almost panicked at the prospect—she wouldn't know the proper protocol—but she calmed when I assured her that such an honor would never be bestowed on the likes of us. I couldn't come up with a better guess so I asked, "Captain's table?"

Kris nodded, looking sullen and then nervous. "I can't believe it. This is so embarrassing."

"I can't believe it either," I said. "Do you not want to go?"

"Yes…I mean no…I mean…of course we should go. How could we refuse? But…"

"What's the big deal, then?"

"You don't have anything to wear," she said.

"I have my suit. It'll be fine," I said.

"No. You don't have any dress shirts."

"What do you mean?"

"They were wrinkled, so I put them in a laundry bag for ironing service. I checked off next-day service on the order slip."

"When did you do that?" I asked.

"Yesterday."

"So then we'll get them today."

"That's the problem," Kris said. My look of confusion prompted her to clarify. "I didn't remember to put them out them until this morning. They won't be back until tomorrow."

I could have stopped her and admitted to ordering the tux, but two things prevented me from doing so. First, I wanted to prolong the ruse. Second, the tux still hadn't been delivered and I was beginning to worry that it never would be.

Kris got on the phone and called Raj. She explained the situation and was assured that there was no problem getting the pressing service upgraded. At least the fall back position was secure. This was getting to be a lot of fun.

Not more than fifteen minutes later, I was in the powder room pondering how to make an inquiry about the tux rental without alerting Kris. I heard a knock at the door. Kris answered it.

"Oh, thank you! You're a lifesaver. What's this?"

"This is the tuxedo, madam," said Raj.

"It's not mine. There must be a mistake," said Kris.

"It is for the mister, madam."

"But he didn't order one." Kris stuck to her guns.

"Take it!" I yelled.

Joining Kris at the door, I saw the sparkle in her eyes. Everything had come together, though we blew $14 to iron shirts I would not wear on this trip. Oh well…

We had lunch in the dining room. I had a Thai dish and some awesome cheesecake. Kris had a melon seafood boat. It took me a while to realize that the waiter who had rushed to serve us at a table that was not normally his responsibility was Bandasak. Though my eyes had uncrossed, memories from the previous evening were still a bit hazy. We got the low down on bingo from the ladies at our table. It sounded as though this was their primary reason for cruising.

The afternoon schedule was full. We did some more touring of the ship, attended a wine tasting in the Savoy Lounge ($8 per person), followed by a rum tasting in the Logo Shop, and a trip to the liquor store to secure a supply of the flavored rums we had just sampled. They would be packed in boxes and delivered to our room on the last night of the cruise.

The wine tasting was interesting. We were seated with two young gentlemen, one of whom was very talkative and already two and a half sheets to the wind. He had just reached the age of majority and, apparently, was making up for lost time. The guys had already polished off the plate of bread, grapes, and cheese supplied for palate cleansing, so we asked for a replacement while explaining its purpose to our tablemates. The event was informative, the wines were good, and we resolved to do the whole thing again. The talkative one stopped sampling and nodded off about halfway through the event. I personally stepped in to prevent his unsampled wines from going to waste.

At 5:00 p.m., it was time for the massage. Nellie (South Africa) and Anna (New Zealand) arrived with their tables and other goodies and set up on the windy verandah. They assured us that it was not too hot for them—they enjoyed getting out for a bit. I set up the portable stereo on the verandah and put on some soothing jazz. For the next hour, oily hands pulled tension from our bodies, leaving us limp and relaxed. We enjoyed talking to Nellie and Anna—they were very friendly and accommodating. We would see them and stop for a chat almost every day during the remainder of the cruise.

I could have ended the day right there and slithered into bed, but it was time to get ready for dinner. According to our invitation, we were supposed to "Meet the social hostess in Rendezvous Square at 8:25 p.m." It was now 6:00, and Kris's hair looked like you'd expect after a day in the howling wind and salt air.

She panicked. I smiled.

My smile at Kris's hair dilemma was, of course, sympathetic. It had no discernible effect in calming her. Each year I have less hair to worry about, and it rarely is a significant factor in preparing for an outing.

Kris decided that she would run over to the salon and plead for mercy. I thought it very unlikely that she would be served on zero notice less than three hours before the captain's welcome dinner, but she was desperate and flew out the door with charge card in hand. I kicked back and tried to slow down a bit.

The day had been hectic, and I was uncertain and a little anxious about what lay ahead. Suddenly it occurred to me that I had missed the gathering of "cruise-critics" scheduled that afternoon in the Stratosphere Lounge. The people chatting about our cruise on the Internet discussion board seemed to concentrate almost exclusively on a cave tubing tour they booked independently for the visit to Belize. I might have felt left out at the gathering since we were going on the Lamanai excursion, but I was sorry I missed the chance to meet the group.

I mixed a G&T in my insulated mug and went to my favorite place, the verandah. This particular drink did not increase my shipboard tab. I admit that I broke the rules and brought a few nips in my luggage. If anyone from Celebrity Cruises reads this, I invite you to review my beverage charges before placing me on the master passenger blacklist. You can't possibly be miffed…

My mind and body refreshed, I belatedly thought it wise to try on the rental tux. I took it out of the bag, and pulled on the pants. I had specified a 29-inch inseam, but these were at least thirty-five inches. Now it was my turn to panic. I called Raj and explained the problem. He was at the door seconds later, peering down first at my face and then to the point where the pants puddled on the floor.

He paused, and then burst into laughter. I had managed to crack his composure. It was a great moment.

"The pants are too long, sir," Raj said when his laughter had subsided.

"Just a bit," I said. "Is there anything we can do?"

"Of course, sir. May I come in, sir?"

I led Raj into the room, and he stooped down to roll the pants legs up to the correct length. Then he waited discreetly in the hallway while I removed the pants and passed them out the door. He assured me, as was his custom, that there was "No problem, sir." I was already a believer in his ability to iron things out, and now I had the chance to test his hemming ability. He took the pants, called a few minutes later to verify the correct length, and had them back to me minutes after that.

I was fully dressed and waiting when Kris returned from her adventure just after seven o'clock. She entered the cabin and there it was again—the sparkle, both eyes this time. Her hair even sparkled, and it was obvious that either the salon had fit her in to the schedule or a freak gust of wind had laid every strand of hair in the correct place. She confirmed the former, saying that the salon personnel were just like everyone else we'd encountered on the staff so far, which is to say, simply fantastic. The salon manager had personally taken her on without hesitation upon hearing the dilemma, and Kris thanked her partially by buying some recommended anti-frizz miracle elixir in a fancy bottle. She handed me the charge slip, and I quickly calculated that we could have purchased 8.8235 of those fancy tropical drinks in the souvenir glasses for the same price. Our collection of two fancy-drink glasses cuddled happily on the desk, and we followed their example—standing on the floor, though.

Kris had to stay indoors because the hair-wrecking wind was still howling outside. I went back out to the verandah while she got dressed. Yes, I peeked—another point in favor of the verandah. Standing out there in a tuxedo, looking at the sea and the first colors of the approaching sunset, made me feel special. The 90-degree air made me feel hot. I wear short sleeves all winter in New Hampshire, so a long-sleeve shirt under a tuxedo jacket made air-conditioning my best friend. I went back inside after a few minutes.

Kris wore a special dress on this night. Her mother made the dress fifty years ago, using lace from the store owned by Kris's great-grandfather. Mom sent it to us just a few weeks earlier, squished into a mailing envelope, reeking of mothballs, and in need of a new zipper. Now, dry-cleaned and tailored, the dress was going out for a night on the town for the first time in decades—only this time, the town was floating.

The gambling money fetched from the safe, we made our way as directed to Rendezvous Square, starboard side, arriving at 8:25 p.m. on the dot. A band was playing, people were drinking and some were dancing, but there was no one at all in the starboard seating area.

"This doesn't look right. Are you sure this is the place?" asked Kris.

I consulted the invitation and my watch. "Yes, I'm sure."

"Are you sure this is the starboard side? Look at all the people on the other side."

"They're on the port side. We're on the starboard side. Port and left both have four characters, that's how I remember."

That seemed to put her at ease. We decided to just stand there and look perplexed until something happened. Our act was well rehearsed by the time a young blond woman in a flowing gown and beaming smile rushed up to greet us a few minute later.

"Hello, Mr. and Mrs. 'X'—so nice to see you again!" the woman exclaimed. "Are you enjoying your cruise?"

We both nodded enthusiastically. "So far, so good," I said.

The woman looked at my forehead. "Oh dear. What happened?" she asked.

I summarized the events surrounding my injury in a few sentences. "No big deal," I concluded.

"Well, you're in for a real treat tonight." The woman directed us to a table in the corner before excusing herself. "I'll be right back with the waitress."

"She seems to know us," I said to Kris.

"Yeah, she looks familiar, but I can't place her," she responded.

You've probably got it all figured out. In New England, there is an expression, "Light dawns on Marblehead." Marblehead is a quaint seaside town in Massachusetts, or in our case, the space from the neck up. It took us several minutes, but we finally realized that this was the woman who took us under her wing at the embarkation. I didn't memorize her name (Liz) until we met her for a third time. I can't remember my own name sometimes, and Kris regularly mixes up our own children's names.

Just as we were placing our drink orders (on the captain, of course), three other couples sauntered up and the introductions began. Joining us were two sets of newlyweds and another couple a bit older than the rest of the group. The small talk began, and we looked for the reason why we, out of all the other passengers, were chosen for this event. Liz rejoined us and said that she did not know the answer. She receives the list from headquarters just before the cruise. That explained some things—she recognized our name at the embarkation and you know the rest. Mystery solved.

Among us, the only common thread we could find was that one member of each couple worked in education—three teachers and an assistant principal. Half of us were in suites, half were newlywed, half were celebrating an anniversary. The other long-wed couple had been selected to dine with the captain on each of their three cruises. They had no idea why this was so, but were clearly the most relaxed among us.

We had time for two drinks before Captain Margaritus arrived. We had already affectionately renamed him "Captain Margarita," a salty old dog to be sure. Kris was drinking champagne—she had somehow acquired a taste for it since our arrival. I continued to deny the cruise line revenue on gin drinks. By this time, 8:45, everyone but our party had been seated in the dining room.

We had another round of introductions for the captain's benefit. The ladies each received a long stem rose before we set out, two by two, toward the upper level dining room entrance.

Kris immediately turned to me and animatedly pointed to her shoes. They were brand new 3-inch spiked-heel models acquired with encouragement from Alex, our friends' hip 17-year-old daughter, the previous week on Cape Cod. Kris rarely wears anything higher than sneakers, and now she was concerned about negotiating the sweeping staircase teetering on those heels in front of 1000 dinner patrons. I could only offer my arm.

Actually, I don't think anyone particularly noticed our arrival. I vaguely recall an announcement introducing the captain and his guests, and maybe the band played "Hail to the Chief" or something, but I concentrated on getting the two of us down the stairs in one piece and took little note. I was more concerned that the scab on my forehead would hold. I had abandoned the bandage because it clashed with the tux.

We passed our regular table, just two away from the captain's, and saw our empty chairs. Bandasak spotted me and, smiling broadly, gave a discreet wave.

As we passed the table, I paused and said, "Save our places, we'll be back tomorrow." Tablemate Alan looked up, puzzled at the voice coming from behind.

We were seated in front of scripted nameplates at the captain's table under the huge window at the stern. The curtains slowly rose to a smattering of applause, and the wait staff swung in to action. There must have been a ratio of 2:1 in favor of staff at this affair. Immediately, two sommeliers raced around and filled everyone's glass with white wine—really good white wine. I nudged Kris to acknowledge the waiter offering her bread from a basket. She reached in and grabbed a piece.

"He was supposed to serve you," I said lightheartedly, pointing out the silver tongs poised to deliver her selection.

"Oops. I'm not used to this kind of thing," said Kris. It was only a minor faux pas, but she turned red—her favorite color.

Now came a challenge. The sound that I thought was just my head throbbing at dinner the night before was even more intrusive at the captain's table. It was so loud that it was difficult to converse. It was as if all of the noise of the propulsion systems and the capacity crowd focused and amplified in this narrow area. That's probably why they make the captain sit there. I started to make small talk with the man, but he could barely hear me above the din. I shouted my questions and strained for the answers. Eventually, I picked up a few tidbits.

The captain has been with the cruise line from the beginning. He works four months on, two months off. His wife and three teenaged daughters live in Greece. This was his second trip on *Galaxy*, and the first on the western Caribbean route. He was previously doing the Alaska gig, and he never saw a tsunami up there. Like you and me, he is concerned about benefits and pensions. In his eyes, one ship is like the next—they all have the same controls and systems. He does not have a private penthouse suite, but I took his claim to sharing quarters on deck three as a joke. He likes the new gas turbine propulsion systems on the new M-class ships, and hopes the bugs are worked out soon. He hosts only one dinner like this per cruise, so we would be his only guests on this trip. Captain's dinner is not his favorite part of the job. No, we could not look at *Galaxy*'s power plant—sorry. We understood. The captain is an A-OK guy.

During the two hours it took to absorb this information, we were wined and dined like never before. As soon as a sip of wine was taken, the glass was topped off. I had escargot as an appetizer and they absolutely melted in my mouth. I considered asking for a breadstick to absorb the delicious butter sauce from the little cups, but since the faux pas count was still comfortably at one, I held back. A pair of waiters hoisted a lady photographer into the air to take a group picture. It would be delivered without charge to our room the following day. "Without charge." I like the way that sounds.

After the salad, little silver cups of sherbet were delivered for palate cleansing. Then the red wine glasses were filled, again with a fine vintage. Kris and I both had Long Island Duck for an entree, crispy skinned and delicious. The wine delivery continued through dessert and coffee, and I have no idea what I ate. Finally, it was over. My scab had held.

Well, we thought it was over. Liz came rushing up before we got away. It was just then I realized that she hadn't been at the table with us, sadly. She told us that a special row was roped off for the captain's guests in the theater, and she hoped to see us there. *Go with the flow*, I thought.

As we passed our regular table again, we stopped for a moment.

"How did you get to do that?" four mouths worded.

"I can't tell you who we really are," I replied, putting as much mystery into my inflection as I could muster.

We walked away, the James Bond fantasy kicking in to high gear with the aid of about $300 worth of wine—each.

We bypassed the mass of women who hadn't figured out the bathroom thing and made our way forward to the theater. We stopped and looked for the ump-teenth time for our embarkation picture and finally found it. It was deposited emphatically into the bin designated for unwanted photos. Kris is famous for being caught by the camera wearing truly weird expressions. They are too quick for the eye to catch, but the camera is unerring. I find it charming.

In the theater, there was indeed a roped-off row—and Kris's rose was our pass-key. All the other couples were already there, as was Liz—ready with another enthusiastic greeting. We fell into our seats and were immediately offered drinks by a waitress. Kris said she'd had quite enough, thanks, and asked for water. I went back to the G&T routine. When the drinks came, the waitress asked for my charge card.

"We're with the captain," I offered.

She was not impressed. "Not included," was her response.

I deflated a notch as I handed over the card and signed the receipt. I could not possibly complain, though I was later assured that the waitress was in error. I guess that evened up the faux pas score: Us 1, Staff 1.

My most distinct memory of the show, a Broadway review, was the size of the bottle of water the waitress brought for Kris. It must have been a gallon, dripping with condensation. Sitting on the drink table, it was so big that it blocked the view of the singers and dancers. I will not critique the show as my judgment was clearly impaired, but we were well entertained. I did think that the fog machine's controls might be stuck in the on position, but it could well have been my vision.

Time flew by, and the house lights came up as the last sip of my drink went down. Kris still had enough water to put out a sizable fire. We looked at each other and smiled. What a great evening.

"Let's get some fresh air," I said as we left the theater. We escaped the surging crowd of people through a nearby doorway leading to the promenade. Outside, the deck was deserted and the breeze was warm. At the railing, we could see and hear the sea rushing by.

"I think I'm starting to enjoy this cruising thing," I said.

"That was unbelievable," said Kris.

"Happy anniversary." I reflexively put my hand in my pants pocket and felt something—the $20 bill. "Do you know what we're going to do now?" I asked Kris.

"Go to sleep?"

It wasn't time for bed, no matter how much it felt like it. I fished the bill from my pocket and waved it around. "Nope. It's time for our first-ever visit to a casino."

"I don't know if I can stay awake," said Kris, "but I'll give it a try."

We staggered to the casino, and I took the first chair I could find. It faced a 25-cent slot machine themed on the *Three Little Pigs*. I fed it the twenty, and hit the cash out button so I could give Kris half of the quarters. She sat next to me at a machine called *Wild and Loose*, or something to that effect. I smirked at the notion.

The little piggies ate my quarters at a steady pace for a few minutes. I wasn't paying a lot of attention—it was simply not possible in my condition—when I heard a screaming, whooping noise. I looked up and saw a row of three pigs under the lighted pay line on my machine. A digital counter on the right was registering a steadily increasing number. Lights were flashing, and people gathered behind me. The counter stopped at 1000. My quarter had just paid $250, the jackpot.

I thought, *With the way the day has gone, I should have expected this.*

I hit the cash out button and quarters flooded into the tray below. The machine ran out of money and we had to summon an attendant to replenish it. He provided me with two buckets, which I filled with the winnings.

There was only one thing left to do to complete the evening's James Bond fantasy. I grabbed Kris away from her "wild and loose" slot machine, and we headed to the cabin carrying the heavy load of quarters. It was late, although I cannot be precise.

I wondered, *Can this cruise get any better?*

The last entry in our journal for this, the first full day of our cruise, is in Kris's handwriting. It reads, "Back to the room for romance."

Question answered: *Affirmative.*

Another Day at Sea

Sunday, July 21

Just before 9:00 a.m. on Sunday, the second full day at sea, an incredible sound woke us abruptly and simultaneously.

"What was *that*?" asked Kris, with fear in her voice.

It took me a moment to come to my senses. "Thunder…I hope."

The room was pitch black, and I stumbled for the curtain pull. Revealed, the morning was dark and ominous. The deck and furnishings were wet, but no rain was falling at the moment.

"Yup, thunder. Looks like we've got a stormy day," I said.

I made the coffee run. I encountered tablemate Mike sitting under an umbrella at a table on the stern, watching the rain showers that seemed to have us completely surrounded. He had been there since sunrise, and said I'd missed a good show.

Back in the room, the phone rang at 9:27 a.m. We filled out a breakfast order and left it hanging on the door the night before, intending to try dining on the verandah. Raj was calling to see if we were ready. He would always do this, three minutes before the requested delivery time. At exactly 9:30, Raj pushed a cart into the room.

"Good morning, sir…madam. It doesn't look like a good morning for breakfast outside," said Raj.

"Sure doesn't," I said. "I guess we'll have to eat in here."

Raj raised the glass coffee table to dining height and with great care set it for breakfast. Tablecloth, linen napkins, an array of silverware, a pitcher of coffee, juices, fruits, jellies and jams, butter, salt and pepper shakers, croissants, and for each of us, an omelet. Kris requested some ingredients in her omelet that were not on the menu. I read that such requests would be honored, and of course, the extras were there. We sat and looked out the large window and ate, in no hurry at all.

We decided to give bingo a whirl. It seemed like a good lazy activity for a lazy morning. We bought the bingo value pack at the entrance to the Savoy

42

Lounge—$30 got us one card for each of three games, and two cards for the snowball jackpot game. The snowball game is designed so that the jackpot keeps rolling over until (usually) the last night, when the game is played until somebody wins. If you win a game and do the bingo dance, you get an extra prize. I was actually relieved when we lost.

Hours melted away. Rain showers were all around, but we somehow avoided sailing through any more of them. By lunchtime, the sun was breaking through, so we got sandwiches at the Oasis Grill and dined out on the stern. A couple of dolphins played in the ship's wake. Suddenly, it was a full-fledged nice day, so we headed back to the cabin to sunbathe.

When we got there, something was different. Out on the verandah, the glass panels under the railing were perfectly transparent. Previously, they looked like they'd been out to sea for a good long time. I looked closely and couldn't understand how they had gotten them so perfectly spotless. Just then, I felt some water hit my face. Strange—the sky was now clear. Peering cautiously over the railing I found that the source of the water was a mechanized spray arm washing the windows of the Oasis Café, just below. It didn't extend to the Sky Deck, and I couldn't see how a machine could have cleaned the verandah windows so perfectly. The mystery really bothered me, but after a while, I quit obsessing.

We set ourselves up for relaxation on the verandah. The wet chair pads had been replaced with clean, dry ones. Everything else had been wiped down. A gentle breeze moderated the 90-degree heat. I fired up the stereo and selected reggae for today's entertainment. With a couple of G&Ts mixed for refreshment, we grabbed our books and settled in to the lounges. A couple of hours later, Kris was snoring and I thought I could see something out on the horizon. I decided to go exploring with the video camera and binoculars.

Now, I must warn you about a devilish little problem involving optical devices in the cruise environment. I can't tell you how many photo opportunities I missed because of lenses fogging up after running to catch an event outdoors. The video camera usually refused to operate for an hour after being taken outside, chiming a humidity alarm and refusing even to load a tape. Many of our still pictures appear to be shot through a thick haze. Very common issues.

If you plan on taping, photographing, or using binoculars outside, I suggest leaving the equipment under cover on the verandah for an hour or two beforehand. I could shorten the recovery time for the video camera by opening it up and leaving it in the sun—and putting the tape in my pocket to warm it up. After twenty minutes, I'd remove and replace the battery to completely reset the camera, and then it would usually work. It was very aggravating to run back to the cabin for the camera and then out to the pool deck to tape the midnight buffet, only to have the camera refuse to operate until after everyone had gone to bed.

The something I saw on the horizon eventually resolved into the city of Miami. I went back to wake Kris from her blissful slumber, and we watched the city's skyline materialize from the haze and become well defined. Our neighbor emerged onto his deck and he described the scene in minute detail to his wife, who remained inside. This was their routine, and I hope she actually made it outside herself at least once.

A while later, we heard the man holding a one-sided conversation. Passengers were asked to turn off their cell phones upon embarkation to avoid interference with the navigational equipment. When land came in to view, the temptation was too much for dozens of people who I saw and heard holding casual conversations with whoever the speed dial could contact. It was obvious that the man was speaking to his elderly mother, and that she was confined and ill. We quietly tiptoed inside to afford him some privacy. He had a good excuse for breaking the rule.

We hit the thalassotherapy pool again and then dressed for dinner. Tonight was informal, meaning jacket and tie for men. Women could wear anything decent—or indecent for that matter. I am not a snappy dresser in real life, but I found dressing for dinner to be a pleasurable part of the cruise experience. It lent an air of sophistication to the whole affair that was entirely appropriate. We were in costume for a 10-day play.

This was the night that Kris discovered the design flaws in the built-in hair dryer. It took almost forty-five minutes to dry her shoulder-length hair, and she could only use the unit after I wrapped it in a face cloth to protect her hands from burns. Celebrity certainly didn't design the thing, but their procurement agent should try the fixtures before outfitting the fleet. Trouble is that if you bring your own, I don't think the outlet in the bathroom can handle the amperage. You'll have to dry your hair at the desk most likely—or maybe you can trade in your souvenir glasses for a session at the salon.

Dinner was nice—much more subdued than the previous evening. We really got the opportunity to watch Bandasak and Joe do their thing. Somehow, they managed to make four tables of diners feel like they had their undivided attention. Bandasak swooped in to unfold the napkin into your lap before you could even consider it. "Good evening, Mr. Chester, Madam Kris." He always had a recommendation and a couple of times warned us off when a dish had not been well received at the early seating. On this night, he said the steaks were coming out overcooked and tough. Nevertheless, two of the group ordered them.

Bandasak must have known the steaks would be sent back, because when they were, he had correctly predicted the second choices and had alternate entrees at the waiters' station ready to serve in seconds. He would deliver a piece of meat and then stand back discretely as it was sliced—to make sure it was cooked as ordered. Joe slipped in and out imperceptibly, keeping glasses full, rearranging the silverware after each course, and sweeping up the crumbs as they fell.

This night, we were offered Celebrity Dressing. Jodie asked what was in it. Joe rattled off the thirteen ingredients without hesitation. Remember the Big Mac ingredients song? I asked him to do it again later for the video camera. Joe and Bandasak knew all of the ingredients in everything—important, they said, to be able to warn people with food allergies. Amazing. Each member of the wait staff gets one *meal* off a week. Otherwise, they work from 6:00 a.m. until the dining room is cleaned and reset after the second dinner seating.

The sommelier for our table, Mike from Bombay, had served us at the captain's table. We perused the wine list and ordered an inexpensive bottle. During the cruise, Mike really worked to learn our taste in wines, and we had a lot of fun learning from him. No one else at the table would take any wine. I felt they were just being polite, so I repeated the offer. No go. A group of assistant maitre d's delivered an anniversary cake to the table and serenaded us. Alan told us that the cake was originally delivered while we were dining with the captain. Our tablemates graciously asked that it be held for our return to the regular table.

We did not feel the need for any more entertainment and retired early. The casino could wait—it owed me nothing. Tomorrow we would step ashore at Key West and we were due in at 7:00 a.m.

Sleep came to me in seconds. That never, ever happens…

Key West

Monday, July 22

You can request an automated wake-up call by pushing some buttons on the phone—no unreliable humans involved, just faultless computers. A metal placard sitting on the nightstand tells you how to do this. It also tells you who to call for various purposes. Raj had an unlisted number but he wrote it down for us. It is also possible to establish a two-way intercom connection from any phone on the ship to your room. The instructions call it the baby-monitoring feature. Since we had no baby along with us we never tried it, but I now wonder if anyone could have listened in. There must have been some trick to keep that from happening.

I had asked the phone to wake me up at 6:00 a.m. because I wanted to watch the docking procedure at Key West. The infallible computer was ten minutes late, but I was up in plenty of time. Outside it was still dark, and the ship was moving very slowly. White lights delineated the nearby shoreline, and we were traveling in a channel marked by red flashing lights on buoys spaced a few hundred feet apart on the starboard side. I remembered the old boating memory aid—red, right, returning—and concluded that Captain Margaritus was going the right way to get into port. Not bad for his first time here.

As we slowly glided along, signs of life began to appear both in the water and on the shore. The sky brightened just a tiny bit, the first indication of sunrise. We began a race to see which would get to Key West first, the sun or the *Galaxy*.

Galaxy won the race, docking several minutes ahead of schedule. Kris was up now, and we watched the huge ship glide ever so gently up to the pier. Many people complain about the noise and vibrations that accompany use of the thrusters during docking. To me it was part of the thrill—not at all objectionable. I suppose if the Marriott felt and sounded like this I'd probably say something, but this is a ship! I could sense the power involved.

At both ends of the ship, small launches appeared. The ship's crew lowered huge ropes to the people in the launches, who then motored slowly toward men waiting on the pier. It took three workers to drag each rope from the launch and loop it over one of the immense stanchions bolted to the dock. Once secured, the ship's crew slowly winched each rope in until it was tight.

At 6:57 a.m., the phone rang. When I answered, Raj asked if we were ready for our seven o'clock breakfast.

"Yes, please." Three minutes later, he wheeled his cart into the room.

"Good morning, sir. Good morning, madam. Did you sleep well?" Raj's sincerity was unquestionable. "This is a much better day for breakfast outside." Out on the verandah he moved the furniture around, placing the table right next to the railing for the best view. He carefully set the table with the now standard breakfast fare.

"Would you like anything else, sir, madam? Nothing? OK, thank you. Please have a very nice day, sir…madam. See you around, sir." Raj always parted with that last phrase. You have to put an Indian accent on it to get the flavor.

Everywhere I went, I heard "sir." The guy vacuuming the stairs at 2:00 a.m. greeted me as "sir", and inquired as to my well-being. Everyone on the staff did. Had I had been knighted by the queen and forgotten about it? Eventually I avoided eye contact just to save all these people the trouble of addressing me. I remembered an episode from years ago when we hosted Norman, a boy from Belfast, for a summer. He and our oldest son, Ryan (about ten at the time), got along like brothers—which is to say they antagonized each other.

One evening Norman said, in his lilting Irish brogue, "And do you know what it is I like best about America?"

"No, what would that be Norman?" I asked.

Again lilting, "Everybody calls me sir!"

"No *sir*!!!" gushed my agitated son from across the room.

Norman smiled broadly and said, "See, I told you so." Clever boy.

We ate breakfast and watched the sun rise. The town slowly came to life, and various tour operators arrived on the dock to prepare their boats. There was a lot of eye rubbing going on down there. It was 7:30 on a Monday morning, after all. As soon as the sun fully emerged above the horizon, the morning went from pleasant to just plain hot.

Kris was signed up for a boat and kayak eco-adventure tour. I booked our shore excursions online before the trip, but for some reason this one had to be booked on board. Kris was supposed to meet the tour group on the dock at 8:15 a.m. She headed out a few minutes early carrying one of the provided beach towels in a little cloth tote bag we found under the life preservers in the closet. She also took one of the disposable waterproof cameras with her—a great invention for water-based excursions. Later that day we found a bigger, nicer vinyl tote bag in an unused drawer—it pays to snoop around in all the nooks and crannies.

I watched from the verandah as Kris strolled down the gangway and stepped on to the dock far below, where she joined a small group of passengers milling around a sign-waving guide. A few minutes later she marched along with the others to a waiting boat, boarded, and sailed off. I hadn't opted for an excursion this day, figuring I'd walk around and see some sights on my own. I took my time packing up my tourist kit and then made my way below.

When you leave the ship, you insert your room card into a reader at the security podium. The ship then has a record of who got off and when, and this can be compared to the list of people who get back on later. To get back on, you must show a photo ID and use your plastic room card. Carryon bags are either x-rayed or hand searched. At Key West, the local police checked IDs at the pier entrance.

Celebrity has a no announcement policy, which we very much appreciated for its contribution to a relaxed atmosphere. They break the policy under three circumstances, at least as far as I could tell. First is the lifeboat drill. Second, on days at sea around the noon hour, *The Voice* chimes in to announce the ship's current position, heading and the weather conditions. At the end of the public service segment, there is a brief infomercial for some shipboard activity. The third instance came minutes after we sailed from each port. A few names would be called and asked to report to the guest relations desk. These people were unaccounted for. Their names appeared on the outbound list but were not present on the inbound register. Either they were watching us from shore, or my friend the slow computer was confused.

On the gangway, the ship's photographers were stopping people for yet another portrait. I managed to evade them using a risky passing maneuver. I already knew what I looked like—just another tourist carrying a camera bag. I walked quickly off the dock and turned around. Finally, I got to look at *Galaxy* from the outside. The embarkation in Baltimore had been so quick I didn't get more than a fleeting glimpse.

Handsome, sleek, lean, classy—nice butt. These first impressions would survive side-by-side comparisons with other ships at subsequent ports. I took out the still camera and aimed. Through the viewfinder, *Galaxy* was lost in a fog. I tried the video camera—*ding, ding, ding*. A humidity error flashed in the viewfinder. I hadn't yet figured out the little tricks you already know about.

I looked up to locate our verandah. What I saw was surprising, but it solved another mystery. Two men were on the verandah next to ours peeling brown paper off something big and flat. Turned upright and fit into place, new Plexiglas was installed below the railing. So *that* was how our glass got so clean. By the end of our voyage, the glass looked as dirty as it had at the beginning. Did they replace the glass every voyage? Did they refurbish the panels or throw them away? I watched the men service two verandahs before I quit obsessing and continued on my journey.

By the time I walked around to the front of the ship and into a waterfront park, the cameras were ready to play. I found lots of subjects. A group of drooping gentlemen sat under a tree, staring at the ground. I think they lived right there. At a long row of phones, *Galaxy* crewmembers spoke in a dozen languages, all saying pretty much the same things to their loved ones back home. Off the port side of the ship, at the bow, was a curious sight. Two men in a little dinghy were preparing to paint the hull. One guy manned the outboard motor, held on to the five-gallon paint bucket, and tried with limited success to steady the rocking boat. The other man was fighting with a roller on a pole at least ten feet long. He would swing it around to dunk it in the paint and then reach as high as he could to take a few swipes at the hull. It was like a Three Stooges routine, and the third stooge was the choppy water. I was certain that if I watched long enough, I would see the boat flip and everything land in the water.

It was only 9:00 a.m., but it was extremely hot in the sun. The shade didn't seem much better, and after walking a block inland I was already soaked with sweat. Ahead, I spotted an oasis under a sign reading: "Information, Air Conditioned." Entering, I sat on a bench and picked up a tourist booklet. The air was brisk, just like home.

The woman behind the counter was dispensing information, and she really knew her stuff. To one man she said, "No, you haven't been able to get turtle soup here for years. They're endangered, you know." To another, "Yes, the bars open early. Just walk straight up Duval Street." To a group, "No, you just missed the Hemingway festival. It ended yesterday. We had 149 look-alikes this year. You should have seen them. My goodness…"

A young woman came in and asked, "Where can I buy a hair dryer?" I knew where she was staying.

"Well, there's the Eckert's and their prices are good," the information lady offered.

"Isn't there a PX at the base?"

The kind woman made several phone calls at the insistence of her customer. I couldn't help but listen in. The base was a $9 taxi ride each way, and the driver would have to drop passengers at the main gate because of security issues. It was a

10-minute walk from the gate to the PX. Yes, the PX should have hair dry-ers—unless they were sold out. I think Eckert's ultimately got the sale.

I had one assignment at this port, and then the time would be mine. I was supposed to find Jimmy Buffett's shop and get the boys some T-shirts. There is a lot of irony behind this. On a hot summer night when our son Ryan was about twelve years old, we were listening to Buffett's song "Cheeseburger in Paradise" on the stereo. Ryan ran around the house closing all the windows. "This is so embarrassing. Somebody might hear your stupid music!" he said. Before the trip, Ryan bragged that he had just been to the Buffett concert in Philadelphia. See, you are a product of your environment. Parrothead...

The information lady directed me to go the same way she sent the bar seeker. I made my way up Duval Street, which was starting to perk up a bit. Conch trains and other tourist conveyances were lined up in every direction. Tourists who should've left the driving to someone else were piloting mopeds and bicycles through the streets and on the sidewalks. I kept alert, lest it be necessary to dive out of their way. After walking less than a block I was again dripping sweat and wishing I had signed up for an air-conditioned bus tour.

Several blocks up Duval Street, I found the shop. It was small and crowded, but offered exactly what I was looking for. "Cheeseburger in Paradise" T-shirts compressed into burger shaped (and sized) metal cans, with cheese and sesame seed details on the wrapper. I got myself a hat.

Back outside, I walked a couple of steps. Darn, I was overheated again and desperately needed fluids. I turned and entered Jimmy Buffet's Margaritaville bar, right next door to the shop. The guy from the information booth had found it all right, and he was not alone by any means. I ordered a usual, just to see what I'd get—no surprise there. Now, drinking at half past ten in the morning might be a warning sign, but when you are on a trip like this there isn't a lot of flexibil-ity in the schedule. I was here, it was now, and I was thirsty—simple as that. There wouldn't be enough time to return once I met up with Kris on the dock at noon, so this was my only chance to say I'd been to Margaritaville. My drink hit the spot.

Thoughts of going to see the Hemingway house evaporated in the heat as soon as I stepped back outside. It was located twice again as far up Duval Street. I decided to just go get a lime, a couple of bottles of tonic water and a newspaper. Scanning the side streets as I headed back toward the dock, I looked in vain for a practical shop. At one establishment, a motorcycle with a V-8 engine stood on display in the doorway. In the window, T-shirts sported clever sayings such as "If you can read this, the wife fell off"—a number of variations for "wife" were offered, not all of them flattering. This was not a practical shop, I assure you.

Finally, I spotted a fine foods store just off the main drag. Once inside, I quickly found everything on my list. I approached the lone checkout with my selections, cash in hand. The cashier was—how do I put this—stunning. Long flowing hair and fluttering lashes, dangling hoop earrings, bright red lipstick, midriff-baring halter-top, and tight pants tapering to high spiked heels. Just as I arrived, he turned to the bagger and the two men started to bicker with each other. I did not dare interrupt. The cashier, who I took to be the store manager or owner, was upset that the bagger was not putting the store's advertising circulars in customers' bags. I listened with amusement for a couple of minutes before the cashier finally noticed me. He continued to berate the bagger while ringing up my order.

As the cashier handed me the change he said, "I'm so sorry to keep you waiting."

"No problem," I replied.

The bagger put my purchases in a plastic bag. When he reached for a store circular, I stopped him. "No thanks," I said. "I'm only here for the day." I smiled politely at the cashier as I left.

I walked some side streets looking at the architecture. I got closer to the ship, catching glimpses of the gleaming lady between and over the buildings. As I rounded the corner by the museum, there she was in all her glory—Kris was marching right toward me, and we almost collided. I veered to the right, and she swept past me in a purposeful stride.

"Hey!" I called. "Kris! *Kris!*" She slowed and looked back, recognition finally registering.

"Oh, hey! What are you doing here?"

"I'm on my anniversary cruise," I said.

"You're early," she said. We weren't due to meet for almost an hour yet.

"That makes two of us. How was your trip?"

"It was kind of like a whale watch—sometimes you see 'em and sometimes you don't. The water was very choppy, so we couldn't really see the bottom where all the good stuff is supposed to be. We didn't see much wildlife on land, either."

"Stick with me next time—I saw plenty," I said.

Kris went on in detail about the excursion. Most people on the tour were young and experienced kayakers, but one couple was much older and had never done this kind of thing. After a rocky start, they were paddling like pros by the time the tour was over. Everyone was proud and gave the couple a round of applause.

"How did you make out?" Kris asked.

"Mission accomplished." I retrieved one of the cheeseburger T-shirts from my bag and showed it to her.

"Oh, that's perfect."

"So, what now?" I asked.

"A little shopping, I guess," Kris replied. "I'm only interested in one store." She handed me a copy of the ship's shopping guide and pointed to a listing for the Blue Cat, a pet emporium. "This looks like a good place."

I'd had a premonition that Kris would want to visit the Blue Cat. I guess you can say that we have pets: One large and one small dog, two medium cats, two parrots and three lesser birds, a rat, and innumerable fish currently tolerate our presence in their home.

"I already know where it is. Follow me."

The store was very close by and we were there in less than a minute. An hour later, we left with two bags full of stuff. I'm sorry to say that despite our care in making selections, the big dog does not like his new hat. Not one little bit...

We were back on board *Galaxy* by noon. At lunch in the dining room, we sat with a newly married couple. They spent the morning snorkeling. "Kind of rough, but good," the man told us. They planned to do the same activity at every port. Bandasak relieved our initial waiter of duty, and made sure we were happy.

We hung out on the verandah for the sail-away, right on time at 2:00 p.m. The captain made a deft 180-degree turn, with the stern appearing to come within fifty feet of the dock as the ship spun about. I haven't mentioned the water color—that beautiful luminescent blue. I hadn't seen it since we left St. Thomas in 1980. We could see the bottom until the thrusters kicked up clouds of sand.

As we sailed slowly out past some lesser islands, Kris and I decided to try the pool. Filled with salt water (as are all bodies of water on the ship, including the thalassotherapy pool), it felt great. The pool area was jumpin'. Waiters hovered in the background, waiting for a sign. Dozens of teenagers took up the front lines in the sun near the water, perfecting their tans. Once out of the water, we went topside to relax in the gentle breeze.

The pool band played on and off, in more ways than one. They were often listenable, but sometimes the guitarist chose to play in a different key than the rest of the band. I don't mean just a wrong note—I mean the whole song. During one of the sets, we opted to return to the verandah and the safety of MP3s (played at low volume in deference to our neighbors). It was a perfect, lazy afternoon.

Dinner on this night called for casual dress, which somehow felt right. We topped off a fine meal with the rest of the anniversary cake, delivered by the maitre d'. I still couldn't give away any wine. After dinner, Kris and I headed to the theater for *Cirque Du Galaxy* featuring the Dalian acrobat group. In one act, four performers costumed as two Chinese dogs did tricks—you've probably seen something similar on television. The show was entertaining and well staged, and we thoroughly enjoyed it. The ship was sailing through some fairly rough water, and we really appreciated the added difficulty of doing acrobatic routines on a moving platform. I think the fog machine might have gotten stuck again, but it highlighted the lasers nicely.

We took the usual $20 to the casino. When we were too tired to continue, we left—with $128.

On this day, we missed *Osmosis Jones* with Bill Murray in the movie theater, a vegetable carving demo, a liquor seminar, and an installment of ultimate team trivia. We were going to need a 20-day cruise.

A little card on the bed reminded us to turn the clocks back an hour tonight. I was puzzling over how to do this to the built-in quacking wall clock—concentrating hard on a solution—when the hands magically moved themselves exactly one hour backward.

Kreskin, you're nothin'…

Cozumel, Mexico: Dolphin Swim
at Xcaret

Tuesday, July 23

We rose early and prepared for Xcaret, which is billed as an eco-archaeological park. Selection of an excursion for Cozumel was difficult, but Xcaret won out in the end because it offered a wide variety of sights and activities, including a dolphin swim. The Mayan ruins at Tulum were tempting, but the transportation time seemed excessive. Various activities on the island of Cozumel were interesting, but no single one seemed sufficient.

Kris tried the whirlpool in the bathtub and found it tame after her experiences in the thalassotherapy pool—but relaxing nonetheless. The ship has a desalinization plant, and the water changes character frequently. Often, the color is strange. Sometimes you can float away on the suds in the shower and other times you can't raise any lather. Drinking water supplied in the pitcher by the room attendant must come from another source, as it is always crystal clear and tasteless.

We packed up the beach towels and cameras and decided to try the Orion Restaurant for breakfast. We had tried all the other options, and there was plenty of time to kill before docking—which I again wanted to observe. There were very few people in the dining room, and we were quickly seated on the upper level near the stern.

This must have been Bandasak's "day" off, as he was nowhere to be seen. We placed our orders. In the interest of expediency, Kris asked for juice and pastries—offered for immediate consumption from trays carried by roaming waiters. I ordered the express breakfast. Meanwhile, people started flowing into the dining room at a good clip. A few minutes after our arrival, Alan and Jodie were seated four tables away. We waited a long time for coffee. The pastry and juice servers were busily tending the new arrivals farther forward in the dining room, and soon disappeared from sight. Kris and I talked about the upcoming day while we waited.

"I'm so excited about the dolphin swim," said Kris. "I've been dreaming about this since childhood."

"You have?" I asked.

"Yeah. Didn't you watch *Flipper* on Saturday mornings? I used to wait all week for Saturday morning. It was the only time we were allowed to watch TV. *Flipper* was my favorite. And *Dobie Gillis…*"

"I liked *Lassie* the best, but *Flipper* was good, too," I said.

"I do feel guilty, though."

Kris was concerned about the exploitative nature of the dolphin swim, but unlike many such programs, the one at Xcaret seemed to be very sensitive and well regarded. Xcaret, by its own declaration, was sensitive about many environmental concerns. Bug spray (not needed) and standard sunscreen (very definitely needed) are not permitted. Environmentally friendly sunscreen is available on site. Kris struggled with the decision, but the chance to swim with dolphins was too powerful an attraction to resist.

The cruise line only offered a generic tour to Xcaret. I had to book the dolphin swim separately on the Internet. The main Xcaret Web site does not offer much information on the dolphin program, but *www.viadelphi.com* is dedicated to the topic and is the place to make reservations. We were instructed to check in and pay for the program ($90 cash or credit card) at the information desk no later than noon for the 1:00 p.m. session.

I noticed that Jodie and Alan were getting up from their table. They were finished with breakfast, and we still had nothing to eat. The starboard windows were suddenly filled with a close-up view of another cruise ship as *Galaxy* slid into her berth at Cozumel. I caught our waiter's attention and made the point that we had been waiting for an exceptionally long time. My fruit and toast arrived promptly thereafter, and the pastry man was summoned for Kris. The ship was early and breakfast was late, so I missed the docking show.

With an increased appreciation of the service from friend Bandasak, we ate quickly and went out onto the promenade. Thirty feet away, a Norwegian Cruise Line (NCL) ship rose in a deck-by-deck competition with *Galaxy*. We looked into the faces of people who were looking into our faces, each curious about the other's vessel. As I've said, *Galaxy* held her own. Past the NCL ship, the whale tail stack of the Carnival *Fantasy* rose above all else. I thought of Jonah and the Whale. All of the people located forward of the stack must be in the whale's belly. Where did that put the people in the stern?

We retrieved our day bags from the cabin, exchanged best wishes with Raj, Muriel and Rey, and went down to the exit on deck three. Turning left on the dock, we immediately saw a man holding an Xcaret sign aloft. He pointed to a ferry sitting directly in front of *Galaxy*, and we got right on. The dock area seemed to be recently constructed, and there were buildings in various stages of completion nearby. Some held shops adorned with banners advertising their wares—diamonds, watches, and tours. Hundreds of people from the three ships in port milled about.

After a few minutes, the ferry departed. Our destination on the mainland, Playa del Carmen, could be seen many miles across the open channel—as could the skyscraping observation tower on the Xcaret grounds. The water in the channel was choppy, and the ferry rose and fell with a regular cadence. A man offered T-shirts for $5, but we resisted the temptation. Our progress seemed slow, though we were mentally prepared for the 45-minute ride. Partway across the channel, a large catamaran ferry passed us—traveling in the opposite direction. A huge rooster tail spit high into the air behind it, and the catamaran was clearly going very fast. As we chugged along, Playa del Carmen got larger and more detailed in the forward view. I could now make out another cruise ship well to the south. Many cruise lines, including Celebrity, used to drop passengers on the mainland for their excursions before going to the island of Cozumel. I wish they still did.

Just when we could see the dock, flanked by white sand beaches, resorts, and the blue-blue water, the catamaran ferry passed us on its return trip. It was fully unloaded by the time we arrived. I was jealous.

Following another sign holder, we marched down the dock, through a pink stucco shopping plaza and then single file down a narrow sidewalk. Around a corner, we entered a dusty parking lot filled with buses. In the row of modern buses stood an anomaly that looked like it was built in the 1940s. It had bug eyes and a 1960s hippie paint job. I expected to see Cheech and Chong inside. There was an open observation platform on the rear, and the painted hubcaps said "Xcaret" to those who could read upside down. The guide invited us to climb in.

Inside, the bus was dark. Heavy curtains blocked all traces of the intense sun. It was air conditioned, nicely upholstered, and quite comfortable. Our guide lifted his microphone and began a lecture that wouldn't end until we were well inside the Xcaret compound. He was very thorough and well spoken, but after my preparatory reading, he wasn't covering any new ground with regards to our destination.

The bus lumbered through narrow streets and onto the highway for the short ride to Xcaret. The guide's talk was occasionally interrupted by the sound of grinding gears. We eventually pulled into a large parking lot full of buses, many of which were just like ours except for minor variations in the paint jobs. We debussed and walked through a stone gate where we were instructed to meet at 4:20 that afternoon, and then into a sweltering mass of humanity waiting to purchase tickets. Our guide walked us around the masses and through a special gate into the park. He was very careful to keep us all together and stopped every fifty feet or so, continuing his lecture. He described everything in great detail—how to read the signs, where to get information, what was in the museum, the importance of good hygiene and hydration, etc., etc., etc.

"Is this guy ever going to let us go?" asked Kris, her impatience growing. It was 11:55 a.m., five minutes before the dolphin swim check-in deadline.

"I don't know. We're supposed to be on our own," I said.

"I only have a few minutes before I lose my spot for the dolphin swim," said Kris, panic creeping into her voice.

We were shepherded into an open plaza where children frolicked under a fountain spraying high into the air. I wanted to make a dash for it to cool off, but the guide was watching us closely. I spotted the check-in desk at the far side of the plaza. At the rate we were going, we'd be there in an hour.

"Look—over there. The dolphin desk is where that big bunch of people are lined up," I said.

"I've got to get over there," Kris said.

"Do you have a credit card with you?"

"Yes."

"Wait until the guide isn't looking…wait…wait…ready…*go!*"

I provided cover while Kris broke off from the group and ran to the check-in line. Our tour guide led the rest of us across the square, pausing several times to dispense more bits of wisdom. When we reached the far side, the guide stopped and gathered us together in a tight knot. He looked the group over carefully. He knew someone was missing, and I wondered what the punishment would be. Several minutes later, he said, "And if you need to check in for the dolphin swim, the desk is back there." Kris rejoined the group, discreetly flashing me a thumbs-up.

We were told all about the underground river. You can don a life jacket and float through a system of caves and caverns while your personal effects are secured and delivered to the exit point. The water is just over 60 degrees Fahrenheit. It must have been over a hundred where we stood. The guide started to lead the group into a cave for a peek at the river. Kris and I walked slowly, and as the group descended into the darkness of the cave, we made a quick U-turn and tried to blend in with the crowd. A safe distance away, we stopped to buy water. The vendors were happy to take American dollars.

There were still a lot of people competing for space on the main promenade, mainly new arrivals getting their bearings. Using our newly learned sign reading skills, we took a side path toward some Mayan ruins and the crowd quickly thinned out. There are minor ruins scattered about Xcaret, as well as some authentic reconstructions. Walking slowly along nicely groomed paths flanked by lush landscaping, we made our way to the dolphinarium. One of two areas where the various dolphin programs are held, this one was surrounded by trees and bisected by a stone bridge. A pavilion on the shore contained changing rooms, knickknacks, and ice cream.

It was almost time for the program to begin, so Kris went to change and hang out in the pavilion. I felt like I was close to heatstroke so I followed the signs leading to the beach. Down the path, I came to a clearing overlooking the second dolphinarium, which is right next to the Caribbean Sea—a beautiful spot. A series of natural saltwater pools lay immediately beyond, and I made a beeline toward them. The path became a curious slalom course, with palm trees growing in a zigzag pattern right down the middle. I got to the water, took off my shirt and sandals, and walked straight in. When the steam stopped rising from my body, I went back and got my sandals. Rough white rocks mixed invisibly but quite tangibly with the pure white sand on the bottom. The temperature was perfect, and I felt human again.

There were very few people in this area. With the crowds at the gate, I was worried that we would be in a crush all day. Not so. Refreshed, I made my way back to watch Kris in the dolphin program. When I got there, Flipper was kissing her on the cheek. I hopped up on the walled side of the stone bridge in the shade of a small tree that grew there, and got the camera rolling. Kris and a dozen others in her group had already received some introductory lessons, and were now going through a series of up-close activities. From my spectator's perch, two activities stood out. The participants lined up in the water and then groups of two and three dolphins leapt straight into the air behind their backs, over their heads and into the water immediately in front. But that was child's play…

Here's the coolest part of the dolphin swim. In turn, each participant lies on their front side in the water, head up, arms out, and feet pointed straight toward the rear. Two dolphins are dispatched. They come up behind the participant, and each animal puts its nose to a foot. In unison, they push—hard and fast. If the person is following directions and arches his or her back a little, they pop up out of the water and fly forward on the dolphin's noses for one hundred feet or more. The dolphins make a fast turn, leap over their rider, and return to the trainer. The looks and squeals produced by the participants are priceless.

When asked to describe her experience Kris used two words, in this order: "Totally awesome." She thought just being in the water with these creatures was enough to satisfy, and didn't really expect all the rest.

During the dolphin swim, a photographer and videographer record the event. By the time you get inside the store, pictures from the session are flashing on several overhead screens. You can order these ($10) and have them in minutes. Kris preordered the video ($30) and it was ready ten minutes after the event. Nice operation. They don't take American Express at the photo desk, so bring Visa or cash.

We were crossing the bridge by 2:40 p.m., and paused to join an iguana that was watching the next group with the dolphins. Inspired by the unrelenting heat, we decided to head for the beach. Snaking back through the curious palm tree slalom we made our way south—and found out where all the people were.

The beach at Xcaret lies mainly around a pair of coves, well sheltered from the open sea. It is a very pretty spot. On this day, the beach was filled with families—presumably local. There were tables and chairs everywhere, occupied by people of all ages who were eating, drinking, and sleeping in the shade and in the sun. We walked around a bit, bought a couple of beers with water chasers, and found two chairs right by the water. Next to us was a treed area with a little pond surrounded by silly looking pink flamingos like you can buy in the K-Mart garden center—only these were real.

We considered our options. There are tons of things to see and do here, but our time was running short already. We plotted a route back to the main entrance that would take us by a few of the attractions. I quickly ran into the water to cool off and it felt so good I considered just staying there for the duration. I vetoed my own idea and we moved on. Past the wildcat area (with no sightings—they must have been in the caves, nice and cool), we went to the butterfly pavilion. A building with glass walls offered a view of a breeding area where butterflies are hatched. Around the corner, we entered a dark cave and emerged into a deep valley at the base of a tall waterfall. Butterflies were everywhere, some the size of bats. A path ran in a circle around the bottom of the valley, and steep steps led to another path ringing the top. A screen high overhead kept the captives from escaping. Everywhere I looked I saw another species.

The clock was ticking so we exited, looped around a replica Mayan village, through the Mayan stadium and into the museum area. We had fifteen minutes left, so we took a quick trip through the aviary. The parrots' squawking made me feel right at home. With five minutes left, we walked past a sign that said "Observation Tower Free Today." That would have been nice, but we never even saw it.

The clock kept ticking—*3*, town square; *2*, admission area; *1*, stone gate; *0*, on the bus. Blast off. Phew.

Bottom line—Xcaret is a beautiful place. The dolphin swim was worth the trip, but it doesn't leave much time for other things. The people who designed and run Xcaret must have studied Disney. At times, I felt like I was walking around Disney's River Country attraction. It was clean and well run. There are many interesting Mayan activities and displays. You could easily spend a couple of days at Xcaret. Five hours is simply not enough.

We left feeling harried but satisfied. The guide continued talking most of the way back to the ferry. I closed my eyes and ears. I remember him inviting us all back to his house, but not much else. I guess he was using the warm and fuzzy approach in an effort to improve his tips. We reversed our arrival process right down to the fast catamaran boarding and leaving before us. The ride back was quite a bit rougher, but Dos Equis beer was available and the T-shirts were half price.

At Cozumel, a fourth ship had docked, adding hundreds more people to the lively mix. We had the time but not the inclination to explore the nearby shops. Instead, we boarded the ship, dumped our stuff in the cabin, and made for the thalassotherapy pool. The thing is a miracle, and we rejuvenated quickly. We hardly noticed as the ship quietly departed Cozumel and sailed south. Ahhhh...

On this night, we chose an alternative dining option—I called for pizza. Tonight, the midnight buffet featured a Mexican theme, and we thought we should make it to at least one of these events. When you finish dinner at 10:30, a midnight buffet is not an appealing idea. A half hour after calling room service, there was a knock at the door. Raj, in his tuxedo and white gloves, entered the cabin carrying a pizza box. What a sight.

"I am *terribly* sorry for the delay, sir," said Raj. "The pizza kitchen is very busy tonight. It seems many people are too tired to go to dinner." I told him it was no problem—but I think he truly felt that he had let us down.

The pizza hit the spot, though I should have ordered two of them. In my description of the day, I didn't mention lunch—another casualty of the tight schedule. After dinner, we went to the Tastings bar for some international coffees, strolled around aimlessly for a while, turned $20 into $24.75 in the casino, and then headed to the pool deck at 11:30 p.m. for an ice carving demonstration. The carver turned a big block of ice into a convincing flying fish in under ten minutes. Cool.

You'd think that a midnight buffet would begin at midnight, but at 11:45 p.m., waiters paraded watermelons carved into fanciful beasts as the pool band signaled the beginning of the feast. During the parade, we ran into Liz again. I asked her to state her name and occupation into the video camera so that if I forgot, I could watch the instant replay. Kris and I heaped a bunch of food onto plates and instinctively headed for the best dining spot on the ship. From the verandah we could still hear the commotion on the pool deck, but we were steps from our bed. The ribs were great.

I didn't even have to concentrate this time to make the wall clock set itself back another hour. In a few hours, we would be in Belize.

Belize: New River Safari to Lamanai

Wednesday, July 24

The tender for Belize City left at 7:15 a.m., so we just had some fruit from the bowl in the room along with coffee from the Oasis. Except for a few grapes, the fruit bowl had gone untouched previously—its contents replaced every couple of days.

There were a lot of teenagers on this cruise, and they always looked like they were having a great time on board the ship. To see them in their natural state one needed only to take an early tender. Here the teens looked sullen as they slumped in their seats, shielding themselves from the morning sunlight. Parents tried to engage them in pep talks about their upcoming cave tube or river cruise adventure, but the teens' reactions defined indifference. I'm sure they eventually perked up.

We took seats on the top deck of the tender, curious to see our new surroundings. Belize City was fairly close, and the tender was relatively fast compared to the one in Cozumel. Within fifteen minutes we were approaching the dock. Besides the 1950s moderne Radisson Hotel, the first thing I noticed was the water color. I expected it to turn bright blue in the shallows near the shore, but it went brown instead. There were no beaches to be seen—only deep water lapping at rock walls.

We pulled up to the dock alongside a very new tourist-oriented building. A broad channel continued inland, passing under a swing bridge and disappearing into the heart of the city. Most of the city's buildings looked like the tired wooden structures you might find off the beaten path somewhere along the Maine coast. We disembarked and were directed through the open core of the tourist building. On the far side of the building, we stepped out onto a sidewalk just as a modern bus pulled up the narrow street and stopped. A number of large coolers were stacked up next to the curb, and a guide dispensed ice-cold water bottles from one of them as we boarded the bus.

We were going to Lamanai, an ancient Mayan site. According to the excursion brochure we were to bus partway, cruise up a river looking at natural things and then tour the Lamanai site. I had visions of a slow boat crammed with hundreds of people straining against the current for a couple of miles. Boring, but I really wanted to see some ruins and Tulum did not make our itinerary. A tour to Xunantunich, another major Mayan site in Belize, was also offered. It actually sounded more interesting, but like Tulum, it was just too far to travel.

The bus departed, swinging past a tiny lighthouse and the tired-looking Radisson. We negotiated a maze of narrow streets never designed for bus traffic. The tour guide got on stage and introduced himself. He was an engaging young prototypical Caribbeanite, with an infectious little laugh that would have been followed naturally by "Fer sure, dude." I suspect he liked the ganja, mon. After our years spent living on St. Thomas, I understood his dialect perfectly. I'd guess that others might have had some difficulty. He tried to teach the group some Creole phrases, with limited success.

Yes, Belize is a third world country. No doubt. With a population of fewer than 300,000, it occupies slightly less land area than does Massachusetts. This makes it one of the least densely populated countries in the Americas.

Down a narrow street where early risers were stretching in front of ramshackle houses, a crude hand-painted sign at eye level to the bus passengers read "Funeral Home." On one side, junk was piled high. On the other, a Plexiglas lean-to displayed the stock of coffins. I missed a great shot because I couldn't get the camera out fast enough. Sickly dogs walked down the sidewalks and lay in the alleys. They do not enjoy the same standard of living as their American relatives.

The guide described the scene to us. He was somewhat apologetic but his message was, "This is where we live, we are working hard to make it better and it is getting better, and we are very nice people." I absolutely believed him. I'll never forget the first time I went into the densely populated residential sections of Charlotte Amalie on St. Thomas. It was shocking, and it made this view of Belize City much less so.

There are three traffic lights in all of Belize, and the one we saw on our way through the city was blinking yellow. The guide pointed out the national football stadium, a dusty fenced area with a couple of rusting bleachers. There were two colleges, each comprised of a single building. Public and church-sponsored schools seemed to be around every corner. Belizeans apparently understand the importance of education in improving their lot. A traffic rotary with many flags in the median led to the main route out of town. These were the highlights of Belize City, and the guide was proud.

Here and there were signs of prosperity. Behind concrete walls stood waterfront enclaves of large homes, but there were still no beaches to be seen. Brand new government housing developments with blocks of simple pastel colored homes alternated with industrial areas obviously housing active businesses.

As we left the city limits we passed the entrance road to the international airport. I think they were preparing to pave it—perhaps for the first time. Nearby, a complex of modern buildings surrounded by barbed wire, antennae, and satellite dishes was described as the operation at the other end of most Internet gambling sites. As the bus continued northward toward the town of Orange Walk, the population thinned out quickly. Belize City used to be the capital, but when the last major hurricane killed 7000 people there, the government established a new center at Belmopan, well inland. Not many people followed. Today Belmopan has a population under 4,000. Belize City is still at the center of the economy, and is home to about 60,000.

Hurricanes come and go, but they leave a permanent mark on places like this. When a house blows down, its splintered remains are used to construct another one. Since the temperature in coastal Belize rarely falls below 60 degrees Fahrenheit, houses don't need to be tightly built. For a lot of people, the shacks you see are a very practical adaptation to the environment. A hurricane is an awesome thing. In 1979, we went through two big ones—David and Frederick—back-to-back on St. Thomas. I will never forget sitting in an interior basement closet for twelve hours holding our months-old son, Ryan, unable to converse with Kris because the wind was too loud. Ryan had two hurricane-shaped cowlicks on his head, a spooky coincidence. We had no electricity or running water for many weeks. Builds character.

In the countryside far inland, many houses were built on stilts. I hadn't detected even the slightest rise in elevation—the highest points of land were the speed bumps across the main highway where it passed through tiny settlements. Many houses built of concrete block were long ago abandoned in a partially finished state, the result of a previous government's failed program to build housing in the countryside. We would sometimes see a very nice house surrounded by decorative fences, attractive landscaping, and SUV's. Who were these people, and what did they do out here?

The air in the bus warmed steadily until the driver pulled over, opened the door, and disappeared. Returning a minute later, he conferred with the guide—who then walked through the bus, opening the emergency hatches in the roof. The driver pulled out a cell phone and started making calls.

Underway again, with the entry door open and a hot breeze blowing through the bus, the guide sheepishly admitted that the air-conditioning was broken and they were trying to get another bus. The driver kept far to the right on the unlined main highway, traveling at about 10 miles per hour. We kept this up for twenty minutes while the guide told stories and the sparse traffic passed us by. I was perfectly comfortable and would have happily gone on at full speed to the destination, but I was not in charge.

The bus again stopped on the side of the road, and the guide directed us down the steps and onto the dry grass. Another bus was parked behind us, its destination sign reading "Just Passing Through." We boarded quickly and the new bus reached cruising velocity without delay. The air was cold. Near the end of the 57-mile trip, a shiny Range Rover passed us. The guide excitedly retrieved his microphone and pointed out the license plate—a jeweled crown, and nothing else—on the vehicle belonging to the head of the government. It cruised right through the crude tollbooth that lay ahead. Over a short bridge, we pulled to the opposite side of the road. The guide handed out more bottled water and said that he could only take eighteen people in his boat. Some of us would have to join another group.

"Should we stick with this guy?" I asked Kris.

"Oh, I don't know…we've been listening to him for more than an hour, and we'll be listening to him on the way back. Why don't we try someone else?"

I thought that was a fine idea. We got off the bus and walked through an open pavilion to the shore of a small cove. A row of boats lined the shore. Two of them looked distinctly sportier than the others, and one of those had plenty of room for us. We climbed aboard and took seats at the rear. The driver-guide was a short young man somewhere in his twenties, a Mayan Indian Spanish mix (Mestizo), crisply dressed. He started an animated shouting match in Spanish with some men on the shore, and I wondered if we had made a good choice. The other boats departed while we motored over to the lone dock and waited for a couple of stragglers.1

The driver-guide introduced himself as Evar. He slowly backed away from the dock, turned the boat around and briefly punched the throttles. Spurred by 400 HP divided between two Yamaha V-6 outboard motors, the boat carrying twenty-five people leapt ahead with great force before settling back down. The passengers were clearly surprised by the show of power, and everyone turned to look at the driver. Evar laughed heartily and said, "Hold on to your hats, everyone."

We navigated out of the little cove, passed through a thick mangrove and emerged onto the main body of the New River—which was barely two boat widths across. Evar again opened the throttles wide, and we popped up on the plane and hit 45 miles per hour in a flash. The river curved and twisted like a road racing course, and Evar banked through the turns with great relish. His eyes and head moved rapidly back and forth, up and down. In the front of the boat, a woman's hat blew off and shot like a rocket toward the rear. Evar's left hand came off the wheel and he snatched the hat in midair without missing a beat. Evar laughed gleefully and passed the hat forward as we leaned around another tight corner. "I told you to hold on to your hat," he shouted. I was right next to him and was probably the only one who could hear his voice above the rushing wind and the scream of twelve cylinders turning at 5000 RPM. I glanced at Kris, and my grin was so big it hurt. So began our slow, boring boat ride. It did get better...

The river widened out just slightly as we continued. Suddenly Evar whipped the wheel to the right and the boat sliced a 180-degree turn at full speed. He cut the throttles and we drifted toward shore. "Iguana," said Evar, and everybody heard him this time. We all looked, but nobody saw anything but trees on the shore. "Up there, on that branch," Evar clarified. He had to take us step-by-step before anybody spotted it. It took me about three minutes.

We traveled almost 30 miles up river like this. We stopped to see Jesus birds walking on water, buzzards hunting for lunch, poisonous trees side by side with trees that excrete the antidote and swarms of yellow butterflies. We heard stories about the Mennonite farmers who are responsible for 95 percent of the agriculture here, pausing at a bend in the river to view a crude but pastoral farm near a settlement called Shipyard.

At length, we burst from the narrow confines of the river into a 3-mile wide bay. On the right was the only hill I'd seen—Lamanai. Ahead of us was the twin to our boat, motoring along at a moderate speed.

"Let's race them," shouted a man sitting in front of Evar. Other passengers joined in the appeal.

"I have better props. It's no contest," Evar shouted back.

The other boat suddenly sped up and Evar decided to rise to the challenge. We overtook the competitor easily before backing off. For a final thrill, Evar turned sharply and crossed the other boat's wake. The passengers screamed with delight as we experienced a moment of weightlessness before splashing down heavily. Ours was the last boat to arrive at the dock. I guess there weren't any slowpokes among the guides.

Evar explained the next phase of our journey. We would have lunch first, and then rejoin him for a walking tour of the ruins. "Oh, I almost forgot," Evar said. "At the end of the tour, they usually give you a drink of Belizean coconut rum. If you mix it with a little pineapple juice, you get a drink called panty ripper." The passengers roared with delight.

At the end of the long dock, a sign welcomed us to Lamanai. We climbed a slight rise to a wooded area containing some simple stone buildings and picnic pavilions. Two lines formed for lunch, which was being dished up by what appeared to be a couple of families—everyone from children on up to grandparents. An older woman chanted to the crowd, "Try my bread. I made it this morning. It is delicious. The tortillas are like gold, so please take one only if you are going to eat it."

I took out my video camera, turned it on, and tucked it under my arm so it was aimed in the direction of the servers. We took our plates and asked for some of everything. Paprika chicken, rice with beans, yellow rice, homemade coleslaw, and fresh bread were dished up by a succession of amiable people. At the end of the serving line, a man wearing his hair tied back in a ponytail was overseeing the last buffet table, which was self-serve. He realized that the video camera made it impossible for me to reach for the goodies.

"May I help you with this, sir?"

"Yes, please," I said, grateful for the assistance.

"These are some chips—some tortilla chips," he said with a jolly laugh as he served a mound of chips. "OK, señor. That's good, or a little more?"

"A little more, please."

"How about some of this—some salsa?"

I nodded vigorously.

"And your coconut tart." The man turned his attention to the next person in line, but the chant of the woman popped into my head. Something was missing.

"May I have the tortilla, please?" I asked.

"Yes, of course," he said, reaching for a container hidden behind the pile of chips. "This is the gold I'm hiding here."

"I knew he was going to ask for one of those," said Kris. This sent the man into another round of gleeful laughter as he carefully laid a tortilla on top of my mountain of food.

The food on *Galaxy* is indeed fine, but chef Roux could stand a lesson from this group. The lunch was delicious, and we ate every scrap. The tortilla was, well—like gold. There wasn't time for seconds, which was most unfortunate.

In my reading before the trip, many people expressed concern about bugs in Belize. I hadn't seen one yet. After lunch we found Evar, who said, "If anybody has bug spray, now is the time to put it on—but you won't need it." A moment later, I heard a mosquito at my ear. I swatted at it, and that was my last contact with a bug of any sort. You should try going outside in New Hampshire in the morning, evening, night, or anytime during the entire month of May—the insects just laugh at feeble measures like bug spray. We had some with us just to be safe, but didn't bother applying it. Maybe there are bugs at Lamanai under certain conditions, but for our trip it was bah, humbug.

"OK, everybody—let's keep to the trails. Remember, it's a jungle out there," said Evar. He then led us up a trail that was quickly enveloped in thick vegetation. We were indeed in a jungle. The transition was swift and striking. As we walked along, Evar began dispensing all kinds of interesting information about the Mayan culture, the history of Lamanai, his own heritage, flora, fauna, folk medicine, and human sacrifice. His knowledge was remarkably deep. When questioned about the extent of it, he told us that tour guides in Belize were licensed only after an intensive period of study and testing.

We stopped under a looming tree. Evar stooped to pick up a large round fruit that had fallen to the ground. "From this we get a natural glue," he said, displaying the object for all to see. "The way that two of them hang," he continued, pointing high into the tree, "the Spaniards called them, in translation, horse balls." The group appreciated another example of his slightly ribald humor.

The ruins were much more significant than I expected, and Evar's explanation of them was fascinating. Lamanai is the site of the longest known unbroken span of Mayan occupation—from 1500 BC until AD 1700 Only a small portion of the site has been excavated since work began in 1974. Approximately 720 structures have been mapped, but only 70 have been partially or fully excavated. Evar treated us to a detailed reading of a Mayan stela, a stone carved with a pictographic historical record describing one ruler's reign. There are unfathomable mysteries at Lamanai, such as the 70 ounces of liquid mercury discovered in a vessel under a tablet on the playing field.

Lamanai, translated, is supposed to mean "submerged crocodile." Evar claimed that when the Spaniards arrived in the 1500s they were unable to pronounce the proper Mayan name for the site, so they settled on Lamanai—a close approximation. According to Evar, the Mayan definition of the adopted word is closer to "drowned bug" than "submerged crocodile."

I took the opportunity to climb to the top of one of the smaller temples, and was rewarded with a sweeping view of the wide bay. Kris opted to walk around the base of the temple for a somewhat less sweeping and sweat-inducing view. I was videotaping her from my high perch when a commotion erupted below. People were excitedly pointing into the trees, calling for others to come and see whatever it was that had gotten them so stirred up. I quickly found the target. A whole family of rare black howler monkeys sat in the canopy, at eye level with my vantage point. A baby howler started performing treetop acrobatics, delighting everyone. Throughout our time at Lamanai, the distinctive call of the howler monkey could be heard above all of the other sounds of the jungle.

At the largest of the temples, excavation and repair are still active. Dozens of men wearing long sleeves, trousers, and hats filled five gallon buckets with mortar and carried them up a hundred feet of narrow steps on the temple's face. The heat of the day was oppressive, but it didn't seem to bother them at all. I, on the other hand, was starting to wilt. On the way back to the boats, Evar stopped to let the children and teenagers climb and swing on vines. I'm not sure how many of them had even heard of Tarzan, but they did a fair imitation. I was grateful for the break—unlike me, the kids all looked much more perky than they had first thing this morning.

Exhausted, we returned to the boat where Kris and I snagged the front-most seats. I aimed the video camera and my face into the refreshing wind, and we raced nonstop back to the starting point 30 miles down river in under forty minutes.

In the pavilion by the cove, local craftspeople had set up their handiwork for sale. A man sold ice-cold local beer for $2. He surely would have sold out even at $10 a bottle. Kris bought a nice hand-carved hardwood bowl marked at $20 and offered for $15. Kris refused to go any lower. Back on the bus with more water, we dozed most of the way back to Belize City. In the open lobby of the pier building, a very young girl sat on a folding chair. She held a cardboard placard pointing the way to a store selling Viagra and other salvations. A tender was waiting, so we climbed aboard and crossed the brown water to the ship.

Many people we talked to expressed major reservations about even stepping foot in Belize. A surprising number of them took what was probably the worst course of action for them—they tendered into town and walked around on their own. Belize is definitely not St. Thomas or Nassau. There are a few shops, but little else in town. It is outside the city where the fun is to be found—doing things you can't do anywhere else. The trip to Lamanai proved to be a great adventure, combining a totally unexpected thrill element with an awe inspiring look at an ancient civilization. The people we met were warm and friendly, and we departed Belize well entertained and a bit smarter about the world.

As *Galaxy* sailed, the shadow of high mountains darkened the horizon to the west and south of Belize City. Francis Ford Coppola owns two resorts out there somewhere. The largest barrier reef in the western hemisphere (second largest in the world) lay out to sea ahead of us. Man's creations are pretty humble after all.

It was another formal night, and we had to rush to get ready for an invitation-only party in the theater. I guess this one was held just for the heck of it. We arrived late, sat down in the front row, and tried to get a waiter's attention. By the time we did, the party was beginning to break up. The waiter returned with a tray full of the party's offerings. Kris opted for the champagne, and I asked for a Mai Tai. The waiter looked around at the thinning crowd and set three of the drinks in front of me. I thanked him profusely.

We had our private photo sitting in the Grand Foyer at 7:25 p.m. A huge crowd spectated. The photographer had a little routine for relaxing his clients. He'd pose us, and at the last minute push my arm down so that my hand was on Kris's rear. Each time, he'd feign impatience at my inability to learn the proper position. The crowd loved it.

Later, as we sat by the photo station sipping coffee, a couple with two little boys arrived for their photo session. They looked familiar, but it took me a while to place them. One evening, or more accurately very early one morning, Kris and I walked through the art gallery. On a bench in the central section, an utterly exhausted mother and her two little boys slept soundly. I was tempted to run back to our cabin for the camera, but dad happened along moments later and roused his family. I will long remember the image, and the same family now waited nearby for their turn with the photographer. The children were decked out in fine white dinner jackets, one in a stroller and the other marginally ambulatory. I asked for and received permission to take a picture while they waited patiently in line. The kids looked great. A few minutes later, when they actually posed for the photographer, the children burst into tears and would not cooperate. I jokingly offered to sell the picture I'd taken (I later mailed them a copy).

Dinner was routine, and we went to the theater afterward to see pianist Elliot Finkel. He was billed as having some credentials, but I couldn't place him. His father plays the grumpy old teacher on the television show *Boston Public*. I would characterize Elliot's onstage persona as an odd fusion of Liberace and Rodney Dangerfield. He was entertaining and I suspected he could really play, but continual sweeping arpeggios up and down the keyboard disguised his ability. On the other hand, the orchestra was cookin'. We wanted to see Elliot's follow-up show of classical and Gershwin pieces, but missed it. I hope he got some respect.

After the show, it was time for bed. The heat of the day had taken a lot out of us. Tomorrow we could relax, but why put off until tomorrow what you can do today? We were looking forward to another day at sea.

A Day at Sea, Cuba Watching

Thursday, July 25

Breakfast and a thundershower arrived simultaneously around 9:00 a.m. Both were light and brief. The sun quickly assumed control of the morning, and we went out on the verandah to pay homage to the endless sea. I went topless, but Kris was more interested in her book. The cheap paperback must have been really, really good.

After three ports in as many days, we were glad for another day at sea. I had no particular expectations or plans, and relaxation seemed like a viable option. Kris, taking a break from her book, held up her hands and said, "Look!" It took a moment, but I realized that in the place previously occupied by chewed nubs there were now genuine fingernails. We had reached a state of vacation nirvana.

The wall clock had stolen one of the hours previously gained during the cruise. I reset my watch, and reviewed the *Galaxy Daily*. We had received yet another invitation, this time for an anniversary party at 11:30 a.m. in the Savoy. We decided to fill the time beforehand at a culinary demonstration.

I like cooking and learned to do it at a young age. My mother often taught piano lessons clustered around the dinner hour when her pupils were free of other obligations, so I was provided with a good learning opportunity. When I married Kris, cooking became a matter of survival. She had not the slightest interest or aptitude, having been completely spoiled by her own mother throughout childhood. I thought women married men like their fathers, not their mothers.

I really wanted to tour the galley while on the cruise, and was disappointed to find that Celebrity affords that chance only to Captain's Club members at the five-voyage level. The demo in Rendezvous Square began at 10:00 a.m. A young girl was recruited from the audience to guest star with the chefs. The routine was well scripted and entertaining, and we came away with a recipe for filet mignon Celebrity. It was here that we learned some of the statistics about running the impressive food preparation operation. Among the more interesting creations were little baskets made of intricately woven potato, served some nights filled with peas or another vegetable. Two chefs labor for six hours to make enough baskets for one meal.

Included in the 800,000 pounds of provisions for this cruise were:

- 21,600 pounds of beef
- 5,040 pounds of lamb
- 11,760 pounds of fish
- 3,250 pounds of lobster
- 21,500 pounds of fresh vegetables
- 2,500 pounds of potatoes
- 16,800 pounds of fresh fruit
- 8650 dozen eggs
- 42,000 tea bags
- 200 bottles of champagne
- 200 bottles of gin
- 10,100 bottles of beer

Were it not for my foresight and consideration, Celebrity would have been short one bottle of gin.

Next was the anniversary party. We arrived at the Savoy Lounge and were directed to stand in front of a display of fancy cakes for a photo. We had dressed from the slob drawer this morning, and wished that we had been a little more thoughtful in our planning. The party was in full swing, and many couples were dancing to the sound of the Celebrity Orchestra. We were seated to the left of the stage before spotting Alan and Jodie on the other side of the room. Their table was full, so we chose to remain at our table for two. A waitress brought champagne, offered with or without a juice mixer. The cake was served straight up.

Champagne is an interesting concoction. I've always liked it because the bubbles do funny things to my sinuses. In all our years together, Kris had expressed a liking for champagne only once—when my sister gave us a bottle of Dom Perignon. Since opening the bottle of champagne in our room upon arrival, she had become a devotee. Between that bottle and the champagne served at the various parties or ordered in the various lounges, I figure we consumed close to 3 percent of the ship's supply for the cruise. I have to doubt the accuracy of the figure they gave us at the culinary demonstration.

The dance floor cleared, and *The Voice* encouraged a round of applause for all of us gathered in the room. I finally put *The Voice* to a face—it belonged to John Howell, the cruise director. He was on the stage and was soon joined by Liz, who we had encountered again earlier that morning. She was rushing to get somewhere important by the looks of it, but screeched to a halt and talked for a long while before continuing her rush at double the velocity. She told us that she was very uncomfortable with being on stage, but that was not obvious now.

I was still beating my head trying to place *The Voice*. The closest I have come is David Sedaris, a very funny writer and NPR commentator. Same tonal quality, but I don't think I've nailed it yet. Mr. Howell has the unenviable job of playing MC at just about every event on the ship, entertaining us while subtly encouraging revenue generation. Many seem to look upon the cruise director as their guide to a good time, but I did not feel the need for his assistance in this regard.

Mr. Howell revealed some statistics about the group gathered at the party. Nine of the thirty-five couples were celebrating their silver anniversary, as we were. Howell asked one couple to come to the stage in recognition of their sixtieth anniversary. By the looks, she in particular, they might have been at the wrong party. Sixtieth birthday seemed much more likely.

In an interview with the couple, *The Voice* went fishing. "This is a tremendous achievement," Howell said, turning to the man. "Is there anything special you'd like to say to your wife while we're here?"

The man was momentarily rendered speechless by stage fright. He gathered his wits and replied, "The same thing I always say. Yes dear, of course dear, anything you say dear." Not the answer that Mr. Howell was expecting, but perhaps sage advice for us all.

I was warmed by the moment, and the champagne helped. I had violated my rule of no drinking before noon more than once on this cruise, and here I was doing it again. I resolved to stick to my rule in the future, but to set my watch one time zone east of wherever we happened to be. That settled, the stage was cleared, *The Voice* declared, "Ladies choice," and the orchestra launched into another number.

I waited patiently to be called to the floor. When no one approached, I cast a look to Kris, eyebrows raised. She looked at the empty dance floor and back at me and said, "I don't want to be the only couple out there." Chicken…

A waiter brought another round as we waited for someone to provide us with enough cover to hide our clumsy excuse for waltzing. It didn't happen, and like most activities on board, this one wrapped up quickly about forty-five minutes after starting. Later that night, I took Kris in my arms and we danced to the piped-in music near the elevators. Nobody saw us.

We had lunch in the Orion Restaurant again. We were seated at a small table with another couple who were already perusing the menu. They would not make eye contact or engage in any way. I checked my zipper and Kris's hair—all seemed in order. After a few minutes the couple stood and departed, saying there was nothing on the menu that appealed to them. This was truly their loss, as I had the best entree of the entire cruise at this meal. The rainbow trout melted in my mouth and was lightly covered in a truly delicious sauce.

As our waiter was pouring coffee, the captain decided to turn left. When the ship turns, it takes a lean like a Cadillac with bad shocks and stays that way for a while. Standing on an angle, the waiter spilled a little coffee over the rim of the cup and onto the saucer. Bandasak was stationed well away from our table, but he witnessed this and rushed over. "I am very sorry, Madam Kris," he said as he whisked the soiled cup and saucer away. When he returned with a clean set, he sent the original waiter away in shame.

After lunch, we went up on deck. Off the starboard side, the hills of a land mass were visible. Except for the shadowy mountains seen upon our departure from Belize, every place on this trip was flat as a pancake. Finally, I could see the shapes that I associated with the Caribbean. The rounded hills marched off into the distance as far as the eye could see. This had to be Cuba. Spectacular cloud formations were building over the land, backlit by the bright sun.

In thinking about Cuba before the trip, I fantasized that some political door would open the island to visitors and we would be diverted there for a historic first visit. Instead, we had to settle for our second visit of the day to the Savoy—this time for another wine tasting. Our sommelier, Mike, assured us that this session would feature different wines than the first. We were seated alone this time, so we had the entire plate of grapes, cheese, and bread to ourselves. I smiled at the memory…

An information booklet is handed out before each wine tasting event. It includes descriptions of all the wines to be served, and plenty of blank space for taking notes. Despite careful planning, we neglected to bring along a pen. When a waiter happened by, I asked if we could get one to jot down bin numbers and impressions. He said, and I quote, "No, sir. I'm sorry, but we do not have any pens."

Until now, I had forgotten about the existence of the word "no." I hadn't heard it in a week—not even from Kris. Shock set in. Suddenly, I empathized with the people whose cruise had been ruined because iced tea was unavailable between 3:00 and 4:00 in the afternoon. I shook my head, and Kris pouted. As I reached for a grape to calm myself, I saw a uniformed arm reach to the table and withdraw. Looking down, I found a small pencil on top of my booklet. We would just have to make due.

Back on deck after assorted wines and bubbly stuff, a breathtaking vista of Cuba filled the southern horizon. We were quite close. An industrial smokestack, ship traffic, and a lighthouse betrayed the location of a large city, which I assumed to be Havana. Roiling storm clouds stole off the coast like refugees headed north to Key West. I ran up to the room and retrieved the camera. It has a panorama setting, and I used it to snap a series of pictures while scanning the island. The resulting picture is 3.5 inches high and 48 inches wide. I think it is a rather stunning sight.

We caught a trivia game in the Stratosphere Lounge. I was preoccupied watching the changing scene outside the window, so the women soundly trounced the men. There are huge binoculars on stands around the edge of the room, but they all seemed to need a good overhaul and were not very useful in looking at Cuba.

We were back in the room in time for tea. Raj was surprised by our presence, and gladly got us some cappuccino to go with the other goodies. Each day at this time he would deliver a silver tray filled with delicious little baked goods. By the time we ordinarily arrived, the hors d'ouvres would also be there—usually finger sandwiches and sometimes caviar. I cannot tell you if the caviar was good or not. I'd never had it before the cruise, and it was too subtle for me to form much of an opinion. What do you expect from someone who has cappuccino at teatime?

I flipped on the TV. A woman who should keep her career options open was struggling for words to describe the activities at tomorrow's destination, Coco Cay. She, like everyone else with one exception, pronounced it Coco *Kay*. I learned back on St. Thomas that the word was pronounced like *key*, not *kay*. I was beginning to get a complex. On screen, a montage of shots showed happy people riding waverunners. I had previously considered this activity, but hadn't booked for several reasons. First, although they look like fun, waverunners are terribly annoying to everyone but their riders. Second, I knew if I ever tried a waverunner, I'd really enjoy it and be tempted to buy one—becoming an annoyance to other people. Third, and in view of the second factor, I do not need another expensive hobby—especially one that uses petroleum fuel and requires tune-ups. The fourth and probably most influential factor was cost. The excursion was expensive, and we really needed to exercise some restraint. We'd be paying for this trip long enough as it was.

As I rehashed all of this in my mind, my thoughts became disjointed. *Kris...dolphins. Chester...waverunners. Fun. Fun. Must have fun...*I flipped over to the excursion-booking channel on the television and hit the book-it key. A block-lettered response informed me that the waverunner excursion was not available. I tried again, with the same result. Kris knew exactly what was going on. She picked up the phone, called the excursion desk and asked if they could possibly fit one more rider into the schedule. She was informed that another session had just been added to the schedule. I could have a turn at 3:00 p.m. My second chance to hear a "no" that would stick had been dashed.

Before dinner, we hit the thalassotherapy pool again. We had it all to ourselves for the entire time. I was tempted to ask at the desk if they would mind drawing the curtains and turning the lights out. Walking back to the cabin, we watched lightning sizzle through the sky over Cuba. It was spectacular. We could see cloud-to-cloud lightning that must have spanned 50 miles or more shoot across the illuminated cloud tops. I went back for the video camera, and Raj cheerily greeted me. I told him what we were seeing outside, and his expression changed completely. "I am afraid of thunderstorms," he confided.

On the way to dinner, we stopped at the excursion desk to finalize the waverunner booking. "Do you want to try it, too?" I asked Kris.

"No, you just go. Have some fun," she answered.

The woman at the desk joined the conversation. "You can both go," she said. "Two people can ride together on the same waverunner."

I glanced at Kris. "We'll see," she said.

I brought the video camera to dinner this evening. I wanted to catch Bandasak and Joe in action, so impressive was their service. We also brought our souvenir wine tasting cups, planning to do a little ritual ceremony with Mike when he delivered a new bottle. Tablemates Mike and Jane skipped dinner this evening, in favor of the midnight buffet. When Bandasak brought out his tray piled high with deserts, I aimed the camera between Alan and Jodie for a shot. Alan looked my way warily, and then began to laugh. His laughter built slowly until it was uncontrolled, and then it spread to Jodie, Kris, and finally me. I'm sure this has happened to everyone at sometime—a total loss of control. Alan mopped his brow with his napkin. Jodie could barely catch her breath and begged everyone to stop. She was laughing so hard she was in pain. Even Bandasak became caught up in it, and he had a silly laugh that prolonged our agony for several minutes. There is no rational explanation for this event—an overdose of happiness, perhaps. Whenever we watch the tape, we end up with tears rolling down our faces. I guess you had to be there.

Our $20 bill cloned itself in the casino before we headed topside to the buffet. It was very windy, and after the mirth-filled dinner, we could only stomach a margarita—no food. The wind worried me. We had really lucked out so far with the weather, but we were smack in the middle of hurricane season. I hadn't seen a forecast in a couple of days, and although the last one said all was quiet in the Atlantic, I knew things could change quickly. Tomorrow was to be our beach day, but I'd heard that the stop at Coco Cay was frequently canceled because rough seas made tendering impractical.

I hadn't been in tropical water in over twenty years, and this stop was important to me. For beach time these days, we usually go to Cape Cod. It's a place where your toes acquire the same color as the water—a cold steel blue-gray. Luckily, you cannot see or feel them until you come ashore.

Coco Cay, Bahamas

Friday, July 26

We were due to anchor off Coco Cay at 10:00 a.m., with passenger transfers beginning at 10:30. When we awoke at a little before 9:00, the ship was stationary. Off the verandah, a small flat island was visible—a couple of squat structures rising above everything else. The sun was winning the battle for dominance, and the seas were sloshing at one to three feet. A ferry carrying staff and supplies was already halfway to the island, and another was loading directly below us.

Raj set breakfast up on the verandah, and we watched the preparations continue. A pair of laughing seagulls hovered off the side of the verandah waiting for a chance to steal our food, but I somehow kept them at bay. When passengers started boarding a ferry before 9:30 a.m., we grabbed the beach bags and a pair of priority embarkation tickets before sprinting to the elevator for a ride to deck three. The tickets were among the many little perks we received for booking a suite, and they allowed us to board any ferry without waiting. I sympathized with the other passengers, who were instructed to wait in the theater for their boarding number to be drawn in a lottery of sorts. We stepped right on to the second boat and arrived on Coco Cay well before 10:00 a.m.

The design of the landing at Coco Cay allowed the two hundred or more passengers to quickly disembark the specially designed ferry. We passed on the opportunity to have our photo taken with the mermaid and continued past some small shelters where vendors were setting up their merchandise. Behind a fabric fence it appeared that a new shopping village was taking shape, and the sounds of construction filled the air. A cluster of wheelchairs and strollers with balloon tires sat empty, waiting for passengers. I stopped at the snorkel rental hut while Kris scouted the beach for an ideal spot.

I found her settled under a palm tree near the end of the beach. Over a sea wall behind us, *Galaxy* glittered in the sun. I dumped the snorkeling gear on the sand, walked straight into the perfect blue water to waist depth, and looked down. Ten toes, all a normal flesh color, stared back at me. I could even feel them.

The mandatory snorkeling orientation was about to begin, so we retrieved the equipment and joined the group. Even those who bring their own equipment must wear a life vest here. The vest is inflated through a mouthpiece, and it can easily be emptied so that you can dive to the bottom without interference.

Pop-Pooof. A woman in the group had gotten ahead of the instructor, and pulled the emergency cord that discharged a tube of carbon dioxide into the vest. We heard that sound throughout the day, as curious people were unable to resist the temptation. The woman was sent to get a replacement vest.

The instructor pointed out the best snorkeling areas. Directly in front of us was a wide shallow area where fish tended to loiter around a couple of plane wrecks and a sunken boat. The lifeguard at an offshore tower would feed the fish upon request. To our left, around the end of the island, lay a much deeper reef. I figured we were good for a half hour of underwater entertainment.

We went straight into the water and snorkeled for almost two hours. In this time, we only covered the shallow area. Rumor had it that the planes had been shot down by the DEA, but unless the bad guys welded supports to the fuselage beforehand, this was not true. The planes were placed here to attract fish, and that they did—thousands of them, in every size, shape, and color combination imaginable.

We were too tired to continue to the deeper area, which is a shame. I imagined it would be closer to my memories of the reefs in the Virgin Islands, somewhat more interesting than the area we did cover. Maybe next time…

Back on the beach, it was lunchtime. People were returning to nearby chairs with food, so we set off to find the source. Under a cluster of trees a short distance away, lines formed at a building housing a grill and buffet. As we waited our turn, aggressive seagulls repeatedly swooped down and grabbed food from anyone who turned away for even a moment. People were regularly excusing themselves to cut in to the line for replacement hamburgers and hot dogs.

The line moved slowly, but we eventually came away equipped with a decent lunch. The burger was a little crispy, but I was not willing to give it up to the gulls. We found a picnic table in the shade of some low-growing trees, which also afforded protection from the screeching birds. Hitchcock would have felt right at home here.

Kris spotted a giant iguana lounging just a few feet away. He was obviously very well fed, but gladly chomped on some lettuce that Kris tossed his way. We had an iguana as a pet once, and he grew to be about four feet long. Guansky, as he was named, lived in the boys' bathroom. When we were in the mood for some fun, we'd send unsuspecting relief-seeking houseguests to use the facility. Then we would sit back and wait for the scream. This amusing activity aside, iguanas do not make very good pets in my opinion.

Near the lunch area, I spotted the waverunner hut and went for a look. A large sign out front displayed a long list of prohibitions for participants:

- No Excessive Speed

- No Wake Jumping

- No Wave Jumping

- No Racing

- Follow the Guide

- Maintain 300-foot Separation

- Etc., etc…

If the sign had been just a little bigger, they would have had room to sum it all up with a simple "No Fun." Maybe this excursion wasn't a good choice, after all. In bold letters, a sensible zero-tolerance policy for riding under the influence caught my eye. I'd just been thinking about a pina colada, but now had reason to dismiss the idea.

Carrying lemonade, Kris and I went back to our encampment. It was already 2:00 p.m., and there really wasn't much time before the waverunner session at 3:00. We sat in the sun for a while, and I took one of the rented floating beach mats into the water for ten minutes of pure relaxation. I'm going to buy one of those things some day. Even though I would carry two of them around for the rest of the day, we never got another chance to float around. During the entire time we sat on the beach, waverunners buzzed annoyingly offshore.

I took a couple of pictures for the record, and it was time to go. "Well, have you decided if you're coming with me?" I asked Kris.

"Oh…I guess so," she answered. "It does look like fun."

We packed everything up and headed to waverunner headquarters. There were convenient shelves available to hold our stuff, beach mats included. The little straps that give your glasses a chance to survive vigorous activity were available at the check-in desk. For a couple of bucks each (on the room card), we made the investment. After an introductory video in an air-conditioned room, we put on life vests and headed for the waverunners. Over my vest, we added a set of straps that provided cushioned handles for Kris to hang on to.

On the dock, we were introduced to our guides—a young man and a younger woman. The male guide said, "Who wants to go fast?" I raised my hand, as did a couple of others. Kris nudged me, but the cushioned life jacket reduced the impact.

"We don't want to go fast," said Kris. I kept my hand raised. "Put your hand down!" She nudged me again.

The guide counted off the go-fast wannabes. "One, two," he said before pointing to us. "Three." He kept going until he reached the eighth and final participant.

"Listen up!" said the guide. "I will go first, and our other guide will go last. You will launch in your assigned order at her signal. We will maintain 300-foot intervals until I stop. You must follow my exact path because there are coral reefs all around. That's why you must ride with a guide while you're here."

Once again, I wondered if we were wise to take this excursion. We could be relaxing on the beach with a cold drink, having fun.

The guide continued with his speech. "When I stop, you should gather with me until everybody catches up. After our first stop, we'll be heading into open ocean. It's pretty rough out there, so there's no way to avoid some jumping. We will forgive you."

Hmmm…this was sounding better.

"We will then go around to the other side of the island and stop for a rest. Ready?"

The group murmured an affirmative, and the guide gave the instruction to start our engines. When all the waverunners were running, he took off and curved toward *Galaxy*, which was anchored well offshore. The follow-up guide pointed to waverunner number one, and blew a whistle. The driver launched smoothly and followed the guide's wake. The whistle sounded again, and waverunner number two took off.

Our turn. I gripped the handlebars tightly, and at the signal hit the gas. We were instantly flying, and I tried to get a feel for what the machine could do. Kris immediately transformed into a backseat driver of the worst sort, shouting warnings and pleading for mercy. "Ahhhhh! Take it easy!!"

Ahead, waverunner number two came to an abrupt halt. I think the girl driving became scared and wanted to let her father take over. I had to make a split second decision, and scanned the water for obstructions. Seeing none, I swung far to the right and gave the sled some more gas, passing the stopped waverunner in an arc at least four hundred feet away.

Kris pulled so hard on the handles attached to my vest that I had to secure myself with the handlebars. From a few inches behind my ear she screamed, "You can't do this! You aren't supposed to pass! Slow down! Don't get so close! Stop!

Wait! Ohhhh…myyyy…Gawwwwd!!" I rolled my eyes and steered back on course behind waverunner number one.

The leader stopped at the entrance to the bay, and we slowed to join him. It took some time for the others to catch up. The guide asked if anyone wanted to change positions in the lineup, and I volunteered for the number two spot. Kris groaned, and increased her handhold. The guide warned us that we were about to leave sheltered waters and go out where the waves were dancing around.

All right, dude, I thought. On the signal, we went.

I watched the guide when he took off, and his technique seemed to be to hold the throttle wide open and hang on. I decided to give it a try. We hit the first wave and launched into the air. The sled slammed back down with the engine shrieking until we got the water equivalent of traction, launching us up the next wave and back into the air. A woman behind me was screaming wildly. Sounded like someone I knew.

We established a regular rhythm: *Bang, whoosh, scream* (engine)—*bang, whoosh, scream* (woman), *bang*…I knew that anyone within earshot would be well and truly annoyed, but this was seriously fun. Huge sprays of water hit me in the face, and my mouth was full of salt. My sunglasses remained fixed in their proper spot, but I desperately needed windshield wipers.

I found that I could establish a less jarring rhythm by timing things a little differently. It was possible to get the waverunner skimming over the wave crests for good distances, but we kept encroaching on the lead rider's space and I'd have to back off. When you let off the throttle there is absolutely no steering control, leaving you at the mercy of other forces. *Faster, please. It is easier that way.*

We rode around the far side of *Galaxy*. I wanted to look, but thought it better to concentrate on keeping the sled upright. The waves became larger and more closely spaced, changing the whole dynamic of the ride. I don't think I ever really discovered the secret to handling the beast, but it was fun to try different approaches to the current situation. Kris eventually became silent. Her face seemed to be burrowing into my neck, and her death grip on the handles continued to pull me slightly off balance. We were making progress. Around the far tip of the island, we entered a calm bay and again paused. Just in time for me—I had been holding on so tightly my hands ached and I had lost my finesse on the throttle. White knuckles contrasted sharply with tanned hands.

"How are you doin' back there?" I asked Kris.

"I'm all right," she answered. "I think I'm getting used to it."

"Do you want to drive?"

"No way!"

As the others slowly filed in, the lead guide dove into the water and came up with a huge starfish. We passed it around while we waited. Kris was carrying a waterproof camera, and another driver offered to snap our picture.

"Did you take any pictures while we were moving?" I asked.

It was a rhetorical question, but she answered anyway. "Are you insane?"

When everyone had gathered, we were again offered the chance to swap places in the running order. I was sorely tempted to put us in the lead position behind the guide, but I deferred out of respect for my passenger. We reversed our route, traveling back over the largest waves where we spent more time in the air than in the water. The kids would be proud. I didn't hear any more human screaming behind me—it was quiet back there. We repeatedly had to slow down to maintain the proper spacing, which became quite an annoyance after a while. The guide did not make an intermediate stop on the return trip, and we soon approached our departure point. As we motored in to the dock Kris said, "I can't believe how slow the first waverunner was going. You should have asked to go first." I rolled my eyes again.

Back on shore, I noted that it was five and a half hours after noon in the next time zone eastward. We had avoided having anything to drink because of the waverunner policy, and shared a strong mutual desire for a pina colada. Floating mats and snorkeling gear safely returned, we set out for the beachfront bar.

Timing is everything, and ours was terrible. The bar had just closed, and the staff was cleaning up. Even though the last ferry didn't leave for an hour yet, there were very few people left on the island. A man sweeping the floor told us that we might be able to get a beer at the hut near the dock. When we got there the crew was packing up, but they were glad to serve us a round of Beck's beer—and then another. Kris ran over to the market area where the vendors were also packing up. She got some end-of-the-day bargains on T-shirts. As 5:30 approached, the last ferry pulled up to the dock, and we went to the end of the short waiting line. Our bags were hand searched in case we had met up with smugglers, and we boarded.

Back on the ship, we paused in the hallway of the third deck to examine large engineering drawings of *Galaxy*. The engine bay is three decks high, and the propeller shafts must be two hundred feet long. No wonder it is noisy at the captain's table. There are elevators and secret passageways in the core areas of the ship behind the doors marked "Crew Only." Our interest in the behind-the-scenes action was piqued. We agreed that Tracy Kidder (*Soul of a New Machine, House,* etc.) should write one of his insightful books about life on board ship. Maybe I'll have to do it...

We talked to the guy vacuuming the stairs. "Yes, sir. Beach days are the worst. We vacuum the whole ship three times to get the sand."

Galaxy raised anchor and departed before we even got back to the cabin. Once there, we took the afternoon's goodies on to the verandah for a bout of relaxation. The sea gulls that had been dogging us all day kept up with the ship for an hour after departure, hoping for one more treat. Around 7:00 p.m., as I returned to the verandah from inside, Kris shushed me and signaled me to stop. My eyes followed as she pointed forward and slightly up. On top of the wall separating our verandah from the neighbor's, a tiny yellow bird sat watching us. Kris crumbled some bread from a leftover finger sandwich onto the table. The bird considered it, but flew instead to the next partition. *Galaxy* must be well-known within the bird community in these parts.

For dinner this night, we had fork-tender rack of lamb. I tried the frog's legs. You could put hot sauce on them and sell them as Buffalo wings—no one would be the wiser. We all discussed the day's activities. Mike went parasailing. He was only up in the air for a few minutes, but enjoyed the experience. Alan and Jodie snorkeled, and like us were painfully sunburned on the backside from floating facedown for so long. Everyone was very tired. Bandasak had a personal favorite on tonight's dessert menu and he brought each of us a sample to try. That meant that some at the table, me included, had three deserts tonight. There were no leftovers.

We went to the theater to see Becky Blaney, who was billed as "The Southern Belle of Comedy Magic." This was her debut evening on board, and for the first ten or fifteen minutes we thought we'd made a big mistake by attending. Kris later told me that she was trying to think of a way to get up and leave without being overly rude. Eventually though, Becky got down to business and became entertaining. By the time we left, the awful opening was a faint memory. In fact, Alan and Jodie went to see her again to try and figure out how some of the tricks were done.

We made our way slowly back to the cabin, both of us ready for sleep. Although I carried a $20 bill, I didn't think I could stay awake with all those hypnotic lights and sounds in the casino. In the room, a familiar sight: The bed turned down, the next day's newsletter on the desk, chocolates on the pillows, and the towels in the bathroom where they belonged. No adorable little folded-towel critters here—this is a classy operation. On the pillow, a cute card featured a child's drawing. Kris collected these every night, and it was only after returning home that we realized the cards were appeals for donations to the Make-a-Wish Foundation. We responded with a check.

We noted something remarkable at dinner, and it was even noticeable in the cabin. With the propulsion systems set to slow speed for the short trip to Nassau, the ship was much quieter. We were due in port early the next morning. We needed to go home with some gifts and decided to sacrifice the short day for shopping. The consensus at the dinner table held that Nassau's straw market was not to be missed. Alan told of striking a hard bargain there on a hat that he bought for $8. He stuck to his offer even as the vendor told him how many hours it had taken her to make the hat. He admitted he felt guilty, but everyone insisted that this was how it was done at the Straw Market.

Kris is not a bargainer. It is for people like her that the Saturn automobile company was created—one price, no haggling. How would she fare in the cut-throat world of the straw market? Hmmm...

I fell asleep thinking about something very important the waverunner guide said: "Coco *Key*."

Nassau, Bahamas

Saturday, July 27

The ship docked very early, before we woke up. Today's show on the verandah featured a narrow spit of land separating the harbor from open water beyond. On it were a few very nice houses, one of which sported a for sale sign. I was tempted to call the realtor. All of the colors you'd expect in a place like this were present—luminescent blue water, lush green vegetation, and pastel buildings. The Atlantis Hotel rose high above its surroundings a relatively short distance away. A parade of boat traffic slipped past *Galaxy*. Raj brought breakfast at 7:00 a.m., and we just sat on the verandah and took it all in.

When we got off the ship at 8:15 a.m., the heat was there waiting for us. Two other ships were in port, but not many people were out and about yet. We wanted to look around while things were still quiet. In an area adjacent to the dock, dozens of cabs and horse drawn carriages waited for business. Drivers who did not have prearranged fares were gathered, ready to practice their persuasion on tourists coming ashore. We were among the first to pass within striking range on this day.

I learned how to say no to cab drivers when we lived on St. Thomas. The same drivers would see me every day, month after month, year upon year, yet they'd always solicit me—"Back to the ship? Tour to Magen's Bay? Coral World?" We befriended a driver named Kenny, who owned one of the big surrey buses. He was a very enterprising man—on weekday evenings he tended bar at our friend's restaurant (The Driftwood Inn). He stayed in his apartment on St. Thomas during the week, and went to his large home on one of the British islands for the weekends. He used his 45-foot cabin cruiser to get there.

We made it through the drivers' gauntlet unscathed, and paused to look at the map. A lone figure approached us. The man was very well dressed and he must have been extremely hot under all those clothes. He started speaking with a very proper British accent. "Allow me to introduce myself, kind people. I am Thomas—a representative of the Ministry of Tourism assigned to welcome visitors to our beautiful island. May I earnestly recommend that you extend your visit beyond the confines of this town to see how Bahamians of all walks live and interact?" It was a great act, but I know that cab drivers don't work for the ministry of anything, and I knew that this guy was a driver.

He had a valid point, though. There is a lot to be seen and learned in places like this. In fact, this relates to what brought me to St. Thomas in 1977. I was a filmmaker in those days, and took a job working on the production of a multimedia show called *The Virgin Islands Adventure.* It took a year to make, and a special theater was constructed for it atop Drake's Passage in Charlotte Amalie. I took the position of technical director and agreed to run the theater operation for the owner. Kris and I married that year, and moved to St. Thomas for our honeymoon.

The show was designed to give tourists a good flavor of the island life and the abundant natural beauty while sitting in a cool place during a 45-minute break from shopping. Most people never see anything other than the Havensight shopping area by the dock and downtown Charlotte Amalie, and that is a shame. From an artistic and technical standpoint, the show was a great success. Unfortunately, the owner refused to make a deal with the cruise companies to be placed on the recommended activity list, and we were doomed shortly after opening. The show ran for about a year—maybe some cruiser out there remembers it.

Tom took our rejection in stride, and admitted that if we changed our minds his was the second cab in line. Straight ahead, a series of government buildings marched inland. We walked among them, reading plaques and smelling flowers. At the octagonal public library, we turned parallel to the waterfront for a walk down the commercial streets. People were being dropped off for their jobs in the shops, bracing for another day of facing people like us. We reached the straw market just as it was opening.

I understand that the market was destroyed by fire in the recent past, and it now resides under tent canopies at the head of Bay Street. The vendors were just taking the covers off their wares, piled high and precariously along narrow rows. I was glad we had come early because the heat was gathering and the tent's air-conditioning was on the fritz—permanently.

We walked past a few vendors who were not yet ready to do business. Kris spotted a hat she liked, and pulled it down to try on. "How much?" she asked.

"Twenty dollars," said the woman operating the stall. We'd have to skip a night in the casino.

"I'll give you $8," countered Kris. I couldn't believe my ears. She was trying tablemate Alan's approach to bargaining. Kris must have really worked up her nerve for this. I pretended not to know her and slowly walked away, gazing at someone else's merchandise. The vendor was not impressed with the offer, and if things got out of control, I didn't want to hear it. I spied a trailer containing restrooms and took advantage of the opportunity to get completely out of earshot.

I encountered a woman washing the floor in the men's room. We greeted each other, and I smiled and waited patiently for her to finish. As I learned in St. Thomas, impatience is a useless concept in the Caribbean. For example, if the supermarket cashier's lunchtime happened to arrive while your order was being rung up, you were fine. If you were the next person in line—the one who had just piled groceries on the conveyer belt—you waited. You were free to converse with the cashier as she opened her lunch bag and laid out her meal. In fact, you could join in if you liked, and were trusted to pay for any goods consumed from your pile. There was no sense in going to another line. It had taken an hour to make it to the cashier in this line, and all the other lines were at least as long. Another twenty minutes spent staying put was the best option.

After a few minutes, the woman finished her mopping and left me to my business. When I rejoined Kris, she was further down the aisle—hatless.

We discussed the need for a new shopping strategy, and reminded ourselves of the power a friendly greeting has in the Caribbean. The first priority in any encounter must be a big and proper "Good morning" (adjust as needed for the time of day), followed by some pleasant small talk. Try it: "Good mahnin'. How are you dis fine day?" The face meeting yours will light up and you will have a new friend. Please note that after dark, "good night" is used as a greeting, not a departing phrase.

Kris spotted an interesting display and stopped for a look. Proper greetings exchanged, the saleswoman became energized and animated. I was assigned to be the model for some inexpensive necklaces and Rasta hats, and the vendor dressed me like I was a Ken doll. As Kris made selections, I kept note of the running total. In the end, it stood at $35. I took a single $20 bill from my pocket and made a show of examining it through the sweat that was now dripping in my eyes. After a moment, the woman said, "Lawd, you two didn't give me any trouble a'tall. That's good enough." She relieved me of the twenty and pushed it into her pocket. "Special first-customer-of-the-day discount for you. Bless you both."

So, a new passive bargaining technique had been proven. I was so hot I had to get out in the open. As further justification, I wanted to get a picture of the three ships in port from a head-on angle. Kris was on a roll now, so we parted company for a while.

I went out the waterfront entrance and turned left. Around the corner stood a multistory office building on land that appeared to stick out into the harbor a little. I thought I could get a good angle on the ships out on the point, but it looked like access could only be gained from within the building. I found the lobby door, and stepped into the air-conditioned space. Ahead, past the elevators, doors led out into a shaded courtyard where I emerged seconds later. There was no sign of life anywhere. At the front of the enclosed space along the water sat a single story commercial building. All of the businesses were closed, and I could not get to the other side where the photo opportunity lay. No problem—I'd just continue down the waterfront and find my angle. I returned to the lobby door and pulled. The door did not move. I gathered my strength and tried again. Nothing. It was locked.

I considered the situation. Commercial office building—non-tourist-oriented storefronts, including a hair salon and a waterfront meeting room—everything dark and locked up tight. This place was clearly a going concern, so where was everyone? Then it hit me. It was Saturday, and I was trapped—maybe until Monday.

No reason to panic, I told myself. *No particular reason to feel that way,* another part of me mocked. I began walking the perimeter of the courtyard. Five stories of windowed walls and a couple of locked doors made the L-shaped office building impenetrable. On another side of the courtyard, a 12-foot iron fence topped by lethal-looking spearheads afforded a view of a trash-strewn vacant lot. The low commercial building along the water separated me from an Alcatraz-style escape—it might be my best chance. I rounded another corner and headed back toward my initial point of entry. This wall was lined with doors, service entries for businesses facing the street. They were all locked.

Desperation was really setting in now. The ship would leave without me, Kris would be in a state of hysteria and I'd fly home on Monday in clothes I'd been wearing for three days. At least I wouldn't freeze to death. I looked around for something I could use to climb on to the roof of the low building. Thirty feet ahead, next to the door for the elevator lobby, stood a large trashcan. Turned on end, it ought to provide me with enough height to scramble on to the roof. As I walked toward it, I passed the last door in the façade of the building. It was glass, but was covered from the inside by black paper so that I could not see what lay within. Small letters on the glass read "Service Entrance, Employees Only." Despite the certain futility of the situation, I tried the handle. The door opened and a rush of conditioned air swept past me.

I stepped in to a small stock area. Through a narrow corridor lined with supplies, I could see a coffee shop ahead. I squeezed between stacks of cups and toilet paper and casually emerged from the stockroom into the public area. The two people behind the counter were quite surprised to see me, and there was no one else in the place.

"Good morning. How are you, today?" I said in my most friendly voice.

"May I help you?" one of the clerks offered.

"Just looking—thanks," I briefly scanned the sparse displays on the wall. Before I had to answer any more questions, I slipped out the front door and quickly walked up the street and around a corner. I stopped and felt a wave of relief pass through my entire body. Across the street stood a McDonald's, a Subway sandwich shop, a Dunkin' Donuts, and a Domino's Pizza. The comfort and safety of the civilized world—I was back.

Past a Hilton Hotel, the trash-strewn lot I'd seen through the fence in my temporary prison offered open access to the waterfront and the view I was seeking. I navigated through the mess, and took the picture. Next door, a beautiful white sand beach sat totally deserted. Oh, how I wished this was a beach day and we were lying in the sun, cold drink in hand. I considered the possibility seriously before I beat a path back down the hot pavement to find Kris at the straw market.

Kris, laden with goodies, emerged from the market just as I walked up. "Hey, how'd you make out?" I asked.

"Great. Look at the beautiful bag I got. They wanted $25 for it, but I pretended I wasn't interested. I got it for $15." The initial "good mahnin'" no doubt clinched the deal. "So, what did you do?"

"Oh, nothing much. Went to a coffee shop, took some pictures, walked around…"

"Do you realize you've been wearing two necklaces the whole time…and a Rasta hat?"

I looked down and confirmed her observation about the necklaces. "No wonder they gave me a funny look in the coffee shop," I said. Kris helped me remove the necklaces, and she dropped them into her new bag. I left the hat on because it worked well as a sweatband.

In a small shop down the street, I bought a Cuban cigar—just because I could. Excursion boats came and went, and the line of taxis stretched halfway down the waterfront. It was too late to do much of anything but shop, so we wandered aimlessly in and out of stores. It was hotter than a Belizean jungle, but at least air-conditioning was always just steps away.

On the main drag, we saw a strange trio sauntering toward us. A man in dreadlocks was walking arm in arm with two well-dressed companions. They were taking their time, laughing and talking casually. I thought they might have been reunited friends or brothers. As they passed, I realized that the two of the men were in uniform, and the other man was handcuffed. Old friends, no doubt...

By 11:30 a.m., we were ready to call it quits. Except for the straw market, the shopping in Nassau seemed pretty ho-hum. Another ship had just arrived, and hundreds of people were streaming off the dock to join the thousands now jockeying for position downtown. We fought the tide and paused briefly to listen to a local band. For the first time on the cruise, we heard someone playing a real steel drum. Others played an electronic imitation, and there is a huge difference. I love the sound. Two gray boats sat at the dock, dwarfed by the cruise ships—the Bahamian Navy, probably in its entirety.

A young boy, no older than ten, approached us offering little wooden flutes for a dollar. Kris knew a good deal when she saw one, and paid full price for one of the dozen the boy was carrying. I later commented that we should have bought his entire stock so he could go spend the day doing something more fun. Kris agreed. You learn by making mistakes.

Back on board *Galaxy*, we went out to the pool to cool down. "I think we're on to something here," I said to Kris.

"Like what?"

"Notice anything different?"

Kris looked around and then it struck her. "There's nobody here."

"Exactly," I said. "Maybe the ship is the place to be on port days."

"This is great. We can each have our own hot tub," said Kris.

"No need to get greedy. Let's share one."

After we emerged thoroughly relaxed from the hot tub, we had lunch at the pool grill. My burger, thicker than those served at Coco Cay, was similarly crunchy. Extra crispy works better for chicken. The fries were very good—take this from a connoisseur.

We sunburned for a while, alternating with dips in the still-empty pool. As the ship's departure time approached, people began to filter in to the pool area. At some point, the pool band started up—disturbing the peace. When the guitarist began playing he was not only in the wrong key, he was playing a different song altogether. I longed for a big reset button. We went back to our cabin for some quiet time, and to watch the departure from the verandah.

Leaving Nassau marked the beginning of the end. It was a very pretty exit. The water was so clear that we could see the bottom at least forty feet down in the channel. After we entered open water, I felt the ship slow. Later someone told me that two people had been left behind and hired a boat to catch up with the ship. I'll bet they were trapped in the courtyard of the commercial building next to the straw market.

We spent the afternoon close to home. Kris eventually dozed off, so I puttered around. Tonight was the last formal dinner, so proper dress in all public areas was requested after 6:00 p.m. Of course, I would comply. In the late afternoon, I wandered down to Michael's Club for the first time—scouting out a location to enjoy my Cuban cigar later in the evening. I entered and picked up a drink and cigar menu to examine the offerings. A group of four or five men sat at a corner table—there were no other patrons. As soon as I entered, the men turned in my direction and abruptly stopped talking. They sat in complete silence for the duration of my visit. I felt like I'd walked in on Tony Soprano and the boys in the back room of the Bada Bing.

From across the room, the bartender quickly approached and leaned in close to my face. "Excuse me, sir. I have to inform you that shorts are not permitted in the club anymore. I'm sorry, this is a new rule and my manager says I have to enforce it. I don't like it, but what can I say?" He shrugged. I had read every word printed in every publication offered to passengers, and would have known and respected this if it was written anywhere. "That's fine, I'll just finish looking at the menu and come back later." The bartender didn't budge. When I looked at him again I sensed that I was expected to comply immediately. Rightly or wrongly, rationally or not, I felt my blood pressure rise and the hair on my arms stand up. I was being thrown out. *Now!*

I left before the security force showed up. In the hallway, I glanced back at the door to make sure I hadn't missed a little sign—maybe a red circle with some boxers in the middle and a big red slash across them, or "Private Party, Intruders Will Be Shot." Nothing. At least he called me sir.

Later, I put the tux on, called Raj for an espresso *and* a cappuccino, retrieved a bootleg nip of Kahlúa from the safe, and accompanied my cigar to the verandah. I had a nice conversation with myself, puffing the cigar while watching the world go by. I had no desire whatsoever to go to Michael's Club. I guess that made it even.

When Sparkly Eyes was ready, we took the long route to the Orion Restaurant and stopped at the martini bar. I had a peppermint martini and Kris had a chocolate one. They sound absurd, but boy were they good.

Gentlemen, let me take this opportunity to strongly suggest that you stop resisting and just find a tux to wear when you cruise. The effect on your SO (significant other) will be amazing—it really means a lot. You cannot hope to understand this phenomenon, so save yourself the agony and quit trying. Besides, I found the tux to be far more comfortable than my best suit, and you don't even have to tie a necktie. The little bow tie clips on!

This was lobster night. Also on the menu were prime rib and a veal dish, among other selections. I asked for a surf and turf, which required no additional explanation to Bandasak. He already knew my preference for medium-rare and did not have to ask. Kris asked for the lobster and the veal. No problem.

As I suspected, the lobster served on board was the southern (Caribbean) variety. To anyone whose only exposure to lobster has been on a cruise, I regret to inform you that you still haven't really eaten it. Compared to northern (Maine) lobster, the southern type is tough and flavorless. Nevertheless, it does provide a vehicle for soaking up large amounts of melted butter, which is half the game anyway.

The assistant maitre d' reminded us of his existence this night by removing the lobster tails from the shells for everyone. Actually, he did appear at the table most nights to inquire about our dining experience and to describe the night's entertainment options. As soon as my lobster tail was gone, Bandasak arrived with the prime rib, cooked to perfection.

I have pretty much neglected any discussion of soups in this story. I'm normally not a big fan but I made it a point to try as many as possible on the cruise. I always got the cold soups. They varied widely in content, but were all enjoyable and at least very good—often excellent. I wish Celebrity would serve a soup sampler at every meal so that one could try them all.

At desert time, the waiters made a grand entrance carrying baked Alaska. Bandasak looked a little embarrassed. I still could not get anyone to sample the wine, and vowed to force the issue tomorrow, the final full day of the cruise.

Tonight featured the presentation of the grand buffet in the Orion Restaurant. A photo and viewing session was scheduled from 11:45 p.m. until 12:15 a.m., at which time the display would be dismantled for consumption. We took our $20 to the casino hoping to fill the empty hour before the buffet. This night the little piggies were hungry, and we were broke in fifteen minutes. We decided to go outside onto the promenade to watch the water rush by in the darkness. This had become kind of a special late night treat for us, and we were usually the only people out there. Tonight, we had company. An Australian woman who worked as a casino croupier was taking a break, and we had a nice chat with her.

Like many ship employees we spoke with, the croupier was working on the ship as part of a plan to get ahead in her own country. She had previously worked in land-based casinos, but preferred the atmosphere on the ship. The stakes in the big casinos were too high, in her opinion, leading to unpleasant situations for all too many patrons.

Whenever we told friends that we were going on a cruise, the most common reaction involved some mention of shuffleboard, which was usually accompanied by a snicker. To date, we hadn't played. Alone now on the deck, we spotted the shuffleboard equipment and a wall plaque describing the game. With me in a tux and Kris in her flowing dress, we started a game. Back and forth, the score stayed close. It was very warm and humid on this night, and when 11:45 rolled around I gladly conceded the game and went back in to cool off. The game is harder than it looks.

We stood in line and moved slowly into the dining room for a look at the buffet. Yes, it was grand. A number of fantastic ice sculptures were dripping their skins, and creatively shaped foods of all sorts packed the tables. Big Jell-O molds shaped like aquariums were detailed down to the imitation fish and plants inside. When we emerged from the dining room, another line was forming for the eating session. Neither of us was interested, especially after the double dinner.

The end of the cruise was closing in fast. Just one more day and night remained. We melted into bed and dreamed of days gone by.

The Last Day at Sea

Sunday, July 28

We let the dreams continue for as long as they wanted and rolled out of bed when the images faded. There was work to be done, but motivation was hard to come by. Coffee was the first order of business, and Raj brought a pitcher full less than a minute after we called. The day was bright and the calm sea stretched off forever in all directions. We sat on the verandah without speaking—all it took was momentary eye contact to communicate everything. This was it, the last day.

When the coffee was gone, we began. I crawled on hands and knees to retrieve the suitcases from their hiding places under the bed and desk. We cleaned out all twenty drawers and started on the closets. I retrieved the tuxedo and began to pack the James Bond imagery back into its vinyl bag. Kris's eyes dimmed just a little as I closed the zipper, but to this day, they remain brighter than before. When we began the cruise, I was exactly the right size for my clothes. When I dressed this morning, it was obvious that one of us had changed. I sleuthed my way into the bathroom and stepped on the scale. I had gained 007 pounds. Kris was up by five.

We both set aside some of our most elastic clothing for the trip home and surveyed the situation. Plenty of room remained in the suitcases, and that simply wouldn't do. A couple of days before the end of the cruise, the sale items began appearing in the ship's stores—so we set out to acquire some filler for the empty space.

We found something close to a mob scene. Extra tables were set up with shirts and bathing suits at half price. Dozens of watches lined a counter top, two for the price of one. The liquor was almost gone. No one in our extended family will need another T-shirt for years to come.

Carrying half a suitcase worth of purchases, we stopped by the photo gallery for one last look. The ship's staff produces a video of each cruise, and it is made available on the last day. I picked one up, along with a couple of dinner pictures that we previously overlooked. If you want to see yourself in the video, you must partake in some of the sillier activities. There are a lot of shots of hand waving staff and cruisers, and some of behind-the-scenes operations. I will use it to supplement my own six hours of recorded material, as there is virtually no overlap.

Back in the cabin, we crammed the new goodies into the suitcases and closed them up. I brought along one of those zip-up portfolios for the important documents. I stuffed it with all the *Galaxy Daily* newsletters, the daily newspapers, the captain's invitation, invitations to numerous other events, a mountain of receipts, postcards, recipes, a souvenir menu, and anything else made of paper that was lying around. I noticed that one of the newsletters was labeled *The Horizon Daily*. Another for the same day was correctly labeled *The Galaxy Daily*. Both were otherwise identical. Someday I'll put the misprint up for auction on eBay.

That was it. We were packed, and it only took about an hour, minus the shopping trip—marginally less than the three months it took to shop and pack everything up in the first place.

We hadn't eaten breakfast, so we strolled to the Orion for one more megalunch. I had risotto fungi and a cold soup made with melon, ginger, and maple—superb. Kris tried a sip of the soup, and ordered a bowl as her second desert. She went for the quiche, but I preserved my manhood with chicken-stuffed pasta shells, peas, and asparagus. A lot of labor went into that meal, and I felt like the pasta when it was over—stuffed that is.

We digested on the verandah and when it got too hot, decided to turn in our stash of quarters at the casino. There were four buckets full, and we labored down the stairs under the load. The casino cashier exchanged the quarters for a paper equivalent weighing a fraction of an ounce. We took our $20 daily casino allocation and spent a long while whittling it down to about $5. We abandoned the games of chance in favor of another relaxing session in the thalassotherapy pool.

This time we were not alone. In fact, we had to wait for someone to get out and make room. Eventually the crowd thinned and the pool worked its magic. There were two basketball pros on the cruise. Sports trivia is not one of my specialties, and I didn't know who they were until someone told me. I wrote down the name of the player I saw once at dinner, but never recorded the name of the dreadlocked one who was now entering the pool. We conversed with him briefly while in line waiting for immigration clearance a day or two earlier, but I did not want to encroach upon his peace now. Later in the locker room he towered over me and said, "I'm gonna miss that thing." I agreed emphatically, and we had a friendly talk. When he left, my neck hurt so much from looking up that I had to spend a few minutes in the sauna.

Out at the service desk I rejoined Kris and we had a farewell talk with Anna and Nellie, the masseuses. I regret that we never went back for the couples' massage training session—but then again, some things are best left to the professionals. Outside, we made a last stop at the pool bar for a pina colada.

"Remember the first day when we stopped here for a pina colada?" I asked.

"Seems like yesterday," said Kris.

"I think we had one here yesterday, too."

"Probably. I remember how windy it was the first time. Hey, your scar is looking better."

I felt the little lump that remained on my forehead, and flushed at the memory. "I'm sure glad things got better after that," I said. "So, what do you think?"

"About what?"

"Cruising."

"I think we made a big mistake not trying it sooner," Kris answered. "I can't believe it's almost over already." I could only agree.

It was time for our inauguration into the cruise tipping ritual. Before the trip, I calculated the total of the suggested tips and stashed the money in a special envelope. For our convenience, labeled tipping envelopes materialized in our cabin on the night before. Kris and I took them and the stash of cash to the verandah. We started to dole out the gratuities and really felt that the amounts were too small for the service we received. I went back inside to get the casino windfall, and we divvied much of it up among the envelopes. It still seemed too little. To complete the ritual, we handed out the envelopes as we said our farewells to everyone during the course of the evening.

The phone rang, and Kris went in to the cabin to answer it. From the verandah, I could hear one side of the conversation.

"Hello…Yes, this is she…Zimbabwe?…No…No, that isn't correct…He's an American citizen…No…No, he's definitely not from Zimbabwe. He's never even been there…I'm positive…He was born in Akron…Ohio…Yes, the United States…You're welcome…No problem…Good-bye."

"What the heck was that about?" I asked, joining Kris inside.

"They wanted you to go downstairs for some immigration thing."

"Why?"

"Because they thought you were from Zimbabwe."

"How did they get that idea?" I asked.

"I don't know."

I thought for a minute, and came up with the explanation. "I know how it happened. When I filled out the online immigration forms, the citizenship field came up with Zimbabwe as the default value. I know I set it correctly, but I'll bet when I went back to recheck the information, it reset to the default. What a strange way to set up the form."

"Well, I straightened them out. You're all set," said Kris.

We prepared for dinner early and set out to just walk around. Much is made in the cruise books of the multimillion dollar art collection integrated into the ship's decor. There is some very weird stuff, but I kept coming back to the giant painting of the woman on the swing in the Grand Foyer. Every time I saw the look on the face of the man depicted looking up (at) her billowing skirts, I had to laugh.

Dinner tonight was very subdued. The pace was slow, and the food was great. Watermelon gazpacho was the cold soup tonight, and it tasted like summer. We reminisced about the cruise with Alan, Jodie, Mike, and Jane. We kept coming back to the sad fact that it was over, so we turned to the subject of conversation to dogs. Clipping a dog's claws can be an adventure. We have to take our big dog to the vet and have him tranquilized. Then, four people hold him down while the job is done. Alan told us that he wears heavy glove-style potholders as protection while Jodie does the clipping. That almost started another uncontrolled laughing fit for the entire table.

I had vowed to get people to share the wine tonight, and they finally cracked. Mike bought a bottle of white to balance the red, and it all disappeared quickly. Mike, the sommelier, presented us with a fresh wine menu in which he had high-lighted all of the vintages we tried during the cruise. After a final orgy of deserts, we stood to leave. We exchanged addresses and e-mails and shook hands in a sad farewell. As we left, I pointed the camera at Bandasak and Joe. They instantly snapped into a practiced pose. Very efficient.

We had $5 worth of loose quarters remaining, so Kris and I stopped at the casino. The little piggies were occupied. Kris went down the line and settled in front of a machine featuring a stampede theme. Above her head was an electronic sign displaying a large dollar amount. This was a progressive slot machine—one linked with several others to offer a common (and larger) jackpot.

I sat at the machine next to Kris. She was carrying the quarters and handed five of them to me—I'm a cheap date. I played one, and then another. On the third play, I got a stampede image in one of the three slot positions. This caused the machine to spin again a few times while making cowboy and running cow noises. For all the racket, I was rewarded with only a few extra plays. They didn't pay off, but at least it was entertaining.

Kris played slowly, using the lever instead of the buttons to spin the wheels. It feels more authentic that way, and makes the money last longer. I had two quarters left, and played one. Another stampede commenced. Three cowboys on horseback lined up on the pay line, and the machine launched into a new level of noisemaking that included bells and sirens. *Jackpot.* I was never going to get rid of my quarters in this place.

A man came up from behind and said, "Awesome. My wife hit for over $1400 a couple of days ago. Too bad you didn't make the progressive bet." Yup, pardner—in order to win the progressive jackpot I had to bet three quarters—way over my limit. My single quarter paid $125, while the progressive jackpot at that moment stood at just under $900. Oh well…

Kris gave me a look—a cross between envy and annoyance.

"What?" I asked.

"It's not fair. How come you always win?" was her response.

"I don't know. Don't let me stop you." I hit the cash out button and filled a bucket with a few pounds of quarters. Kris played the remainder of the original $5 and was broke in a few minutes.

"That's it. I give up," Kris said in frustration.

"I'll give you five more quarters if you want to keep going." I got the look again. I lugged the bucket of quarters to the cashier and exchanged them for paper money.

When I rejoined Kris she said, "Too bad they don't have a Powerball vending machine. With your luck, you should buy a ticket." As we left the casino I looked around for such a machine, but there was none. Too bad…

We ran back up to the cabin at 11:15 p.m. and put the large suitcases in the hallway for pickup. Raj came by and we asked him if we could get breakfast in the room the following morning. For the first time, he hesitated. "Well, we are not supposed to do that. We have to get ready for the new passengers." After another moment, he pulled an order card off the desk and said, "Here, just tell me what you want. It is my job to make you happy." We selected a few easy and non-messy items.

Two boxes of liquor bottles had been delivered, and they were sitting on the love seat. I hadn't factored them in when considering the load we'd have to carry the next day, and they were heavy and bulky enough to be a considerable burden. I would have secured the boxes together, but the duct tape was already packed.

When we left the cabin, we found Muriel and Rey in the hallway. We distributed the tip envelopes and thanked them for their attentiveness before exchanging good-byes.

For the remainder of the evening, we wandered from place to place sampling the varied atmospheres of the evening haunts. Around 1:00 a.m., we made it to the Stratosphere—literally. I'm not big on the disco scene, but the lounge was on the way to the cabin so we stopped in. The dance floor was full and the DJ was spinning the Bee Gees, creating a classic scene. I thought we might go out and try to recreate the dance scene from the movie *Airplane!*, but Kris didn't want to show off. Instead, we made our way to the uncrowded periphery on the port side and ordered a pair of Planter's Punches.

I became aware of lights outside—a lot of them strung in a narrow strip extending as far as I could see. Either we were coming closer to them, or they were aiming for us.

"We're really close to land," I said to Kris.

"Sure looks like it. Are we supposed to get in to Baltimore so soon?"

"We should be hours away from Baltimore. It must be the coast of Virginia," I answered.

Suddenly the lights curved sharply in our direction, alarmingly close now. I stood and peered across the crowded lounge and out the other side of the ship—where I saw more lights marching off into the distance.

"Whatever it is, we're heading straight toward it," I said. I was convinced that impact was imminent, and braced myself against the table. Suddenly, lights filled the windows on both sides of the lounge. The ship seemed to slice right through the lighted land mass and then passed back into darkness. "What the heck was that?" I struggled to decode what we'd just seen and arrived at the only logical explanation available. We had just passed over a short tunnel segment in the Chesapeake Bay Bridge-Tunnel. I was surprised that we were so close to Baltimore already. We could coast the rest of the way.

Kris and I went down one deck to walk around the pool before returning to our cabin. In the elevator lobby, we found a couple examining a big map of our route. Glancing to the right, my nemesis the automatic door stood a few feet away. I wonder if the map distracted me that afternoon. I had no memory of seeing it in this location, but a good map is the sort of thing that would draw my attention from important activities—like walking. I'll never know.

"Was that the bridge we just passed?" I asked the couple.

The man replied, "We've crossed it many times and know the exact spot. We've been waiting out here all night to see it. Pretty cool, eh?"

I agreed that it was, indeed, pretty cool.

There was no point in resisting now. This cruise was over. Tomorrow we had to vacate the room by 8:30 a.m. and join in what was sure to be a nightmare—the disembarkation. In all my reading, this process seemed to be so universally reviled that I was surprised anyone would cruise with the prospect of facing it at the end. Were the previous ten days worth it? We'd know soon enough…

Disembarkation

Monday, July 29

A melodic warble woke me from a sound sleep at 6:57 a.m. and I fumbled to find the phone—taking a moment to peel my lips apart so I could speak when I answered. My mouth still tasted like the water off Coco Cay and my eyes were glued shut. When I thought I could manage speech, I picked up the receiver. My "Hello" was understandable, but not distinct.

Raj was on the line. "Good morning, sir. Are you ready for your breakfast?"

"Thuer," was the closest my mouth could come to saying "sure." I knew by experience that we had exactly three minutes before a knock at the door would signal the arrival of the food. I started to swing my feet to the floor. The room was pitch black behind the dark curtains. *Knock, knock, knock.* It had been exactly three seconds this time—Raj was in a hurry. I covered the still-sleeping Kris and stumbled toward the point where the knocking sound originated. I pulled a bathrobe on over my birthday suit and opened the door. Light from the hallway spilled in and hurt my eyes.

Raj peered into the room and smiled. "May I come in, sir? Is it OK?"

"Thuer."

He entered and opened the curtains just a crack so he could see where to set the tray. When that was done, he turned to me and offered his hand. He spoke very quietly so as not to wake Kris. "I really hope you will come back and stay with me again very soon, sir. See you around, sir." Raj is a man of few words, but he has some towering ideas.

"I thuer hope tho, too." With that, we said our final good-byes and Raj departed.

I showered and dressed, and Kris followed my example. We ate on the verandah as the ship approached civilization. We were supposed to dock at 10:00 a.m. but we had to be very close at this point. *Galaxy* was traveling quite slowly, and industrial buildings lined the shore a few hundred feet away. When I made the bus arrangements with Celebrity, they advised that we would be dropped off at the McDonald's between 3:30 and 4:00 p.m., which meant we'd probably get off the ship sometime after noon.

Suddenly we were right next to the dock. I didn't see it coming. Neither did the captain of the large cargo ship that knocked over a $7 million, 750-ton crane a day or two earlier. The ship's newspaper featured a little article about it and now there it was right in front of us. The crane lay peacefully on its back, and a big chunk of the dock's wall was missing. The verandah gave us one last little show.

The ship docked and the action below started immediately. Forklifts sped back and forth, hauling luggage to the terminal and trash to the dumpsters. Others began loading provisions for the departure scheduled later that day. The dogs were back sniffing around, and the police boat was making the rounds.

I did not keep notes today—the little journal was packed deep inside a suitcase somewhere. All of the above happened before we had to vacate the room, so we were docked far ahead of schedule. At exactly 8:30 a.m., we loaded ourselves up like pack mules and left Suite 1228 for the last time. I checked all the nooks and crannies a hundred times, but I'm sure something belonging to us remained behind. How do you pack up a part of your soul?

We clutched the stubs from our luggage tags. They were light blue, each marked with the numeral one. Our instructions indicated that we should wait in the Celebrity Theater for the announcement of our tag color, at which time we would be able to disembark.

With the addition of the liquor boxes, we both had a large and awkward load. Making our way forward, we merged with others in a slow procession. I could almost hear the dirge in my head. Faces were somber, postures deflated. Many appeared to have made similar miscalculations about the baggage, and we had to pause occasionally as people stopped ahead of us to rearrange their loads.

The wandering mourners eventually reached the theater, where a great mass of people was already gathered. Many of them sat on the staircases leading into the seating area. We (and many others) had to carefully step through and around them as we peered through our awkwardly balanced baggage. In my mind I stepped on a couple just to hear them squeal, but in reality, I was careful not to.

Kris and I claimed a cozy arrangement of table, chairs, and a couch up in the balcony. A giant image of CNN was being projected onto a screen on the stage. I think this may have been part of our reindoctrination program for rejoining the world outside. The news wasn't good. Wall Street was in decline again, pushing our retirement date out another few years. Shocking things happened to innocent little girls while we were away, and I felt ashamed for humanity.

When comfortably settled, Kris kicked back with her book. I filled out the Customs form and went to stand in line to pay the duty on the extra liquor we were taking home. I calculated that our eight bottles (six more than the duty-free limit) should mean about a $12 payment, keeping the overall package cost in the good deal range. Immediately outside the theater lobby, I joined the line that was forming for Customs. Agents were due in the card room at 9:00 a.m. They were a couple of minutes late, but the line moved quickly once the agents settled in.

At the door to the card room, a Celebrity employee let me enter when one of the four agents became free. Each had a cash box, and the agent waving me over had just made a killing judging by the wad of bills she was filing away. I put on my most upstanding-citizen countenance and marched up to desk. The agent hit me with a pleasant greeting and a smile before I had a chance to deploy anything similar. She had the advantage. *Oh, oh...*

In my pocket, a wad of dollar bills sat ready to sacrifice themselves for the good of the country. I tried not to appear nervous as the agent looked over my list of purchases. Apart from the liquor, the value of our purchases didn't come anywhere near the duty trigger point, but I was concerned that I might have miscounted the souvenir T-shirts and that a specially trained dog would sniff them out in our baggage. I didn't want to go to prison over a piece of cloth that read, "All They Brought Me From The Bahamas Was This Lousy T-Shirt."

The Custom's agent carefully scrutinized my list. "Did you have a good trip?" she asked.

Ah, very clever—trying to trip me up with tricky questions. I picked my response carefully, not wanting to give her any openings. "Fantastic," was my reply.

The agent flipped my form back over and lifted a red pen. I inhaled sharply. She wrote something in a bold, bloody script across the face of the form and handed it to me. Then she said, "Thank you, sir. Have a wonderful day."

I glanced at the form, and in red letters it said, "No Duty." I was paralyzed. I owed $12 and I wasn't going to move until somebody took it from me.

As I lingered, the Custom's agent spoke. "Just hand the form to the officers on your way off the ship. You're all set."

"But...I have eight bottles."

"That's OK. You don't owe any duty. You're allowed five bottles each."

I now had a direct quote from an agent in case I was challenged. I thanked her and left the room. The liquor store was nearby, and I walked up to the window and peered in. Just as I thought, there was a sign stating that duty was owed on any amount of liquor over one bottle per person. Later I confirmed that

The Galaxy Daily said the same thing. I could only conclude that the agent thought I was cute.

I fought my way back up the theater's steps to find Kris. Even more people had settled there. I thought about it. These folks were willing to sit on the uncomfortable stairs for hours, just so they would be a few yards ahead of people seated inside the theater whenever their color was called to disembark. They looked miserable. Some of them were just staring blankly into space, but others looked disgruntled—I presume because it was going to take a long time for them to get out of a place they all really wanted to stay in. Mr. Spock would have gone onto overload trying to analyze this one. Dr. Spock wouldn't have fared any better. I decided not to play the game. I was still on the ship, there were plenty of things to do, and I didn't care if they ever called my color. I wanted to get off last!

So far, announcements had been made for the disembarkation of passengers needing special assistance and for those with early flights. Kris asked me to watch the bags while she walked around a bit. As soon as she returned, I grabbed my camera bag and went out onto the promenade.

A small number of people had the right idea. They were out on the deck playing shuffleboard or lounging in chairs with their books. I climbed up to the top deck and then down again, just to see what was happening. Off the port side, a huge barge was pumping fuel into *Galaxy's* belly. On the rear portion of deck twelve, the ping-pong table was in use—as it always seemed to be. Some kids were dribbling around the basketball court. The Oasis Café was serving food. The art gallery was showing art. The coffee bar was—well, you get the idea.

I headed back to share my opinion with Kris that we could make a great day out of this wait. As I entered the theater, a voice (not *The Voice)* on the PA system announced, "Light blue, number one, may now proceed to the..."

My heart leapt into my throat and a voice in my head yelled, *No! Not us—we don't want to get off yet. Pick somebody on the stairs!* The announcer didn't hear me, and repeated the message.

I scurried up the stairs, recklessly this time, to find Kris. She was slipping her book into her bag and looked up as I approached. It was another one of those moments when words were not necessary.

Down the stairs to the Grand Foyer we went. I handed my customs form to a uniformed agent and waited to be challenged. When it didn't happen, I let go—nothing was going to keep us on board now.

Down into the sweltering heat we marched, crossing the dock into the terminal where the baggage was neatly lined up by tag color. It only took a couple of minutes to find our nondescript luggage in the mass and we hauled it to the front side of the building. The relatively few porters were busy, and it looked like aggression would be required to get one. I went outside to see how far we would have to carry everything. The bus was right around the corner—two hundred feet, max.

I went back inside the terminal building prepared to make a couple of trips with the luggage. I found Kris talking with two other women who I recognized from the bus. The women had somehow secured a porter and were glad to share, so we piled everything onto his large cart and headed out.

Henry spotted us and waved as we rounded the corner. He has a great memory for faces, I'd say. We were the first to arrive for the return trip, and our luggage was quickly secured in the cargo hold. Henry opened up the bus and invited us to get comfortable in the air-conditioned space.

My watch read 10:15 a.m. We had just experienced a cruiser's dream disembarkation, and it was fully consistent with the entire experience. It just didn't feel like a cause for joy. Kris was happily reading her book, but I didn't feel like sitting on the bus. I went back outside to watch the shore operation. I hung out with man who was guarding the truck entrance, and he seemed glad to have someone to talk to—all I had to do was listen. Two casually dressed men pulled up in a monster SUV and flashed FBI badges to the guard. He allowed them to park by the gate, and the agents went inside. During our short walk to the bus, Kris told me that she saw a group of passengers segregated from the rest inside the terminal, and that a dog was examining their baggage. I wondered if there was a big bust in progress.

I never got to see what, if anything, happened. By a few minutes past 11:00 a.m., all of the passengers had arrived and Henry waved me over to the bus. A Celebrity representative hopped on board for a minute to make sure we were all satisfied, and the consensus was universally favorable. He told us that a couple of spaces were available on the departing cruise. American Express would have been glad to front me the money, but we were forced to pass on the offer. We were on the road by 11:15.

Northbound traffic moved quickly—there was no traffic jam like the one we saw ten days earlier. The bus rolled into the McDonald's parking lot at 1:00 p.m. sharp. Henry unloaded our bags, we thanked him, and the bus pulled away leaving us in a cloud of diesel smoke. There we stood, on a side street with a ton of baggage in 95-degree heat—three hours before Ryan was due to pick us up.

I went into McDonald's and asked to change a dollar into quarters so I could use the pay phone. The manager said, "We don't have any quarters." A likely story...

It took about twenty minutes to make a 50-cent call using a credit card. The payphone hung off the side of the restaurant, right in the drive-thru lane. I had to stay flattened against the wall to avoid being run over by people craving their Big Mac and fries. Finally, I got through to Ryan's apartment. His roommate relayed a message: "Ryan is running late. He said that you should call this number..." I tried the alternate number, but spoke only to an answering machine.

Kris was still standing on the opposite side of the street, surrounded by a mountain of luggage. I snaked my way between the cars in the drive-thru and rejoined her.

"Well?" she asked.

"I can't reach him. His roommate says he hasn't come back yet, but he called and left another number for us."

"And?"

"Answering machine. It must be for his cell phone."

"So now what do we do?" Kris asked.

"I guess we stand here for three or four hours." I knew that wasn't a good idea. Before Kris could point it out, I offered an alternative. "Or, I could try to get us a room at the hotel."

"Might as well...I really don't feel like driving all the way back to New Hampshire tonight."

"Me neither." In my best Schwarzenegger voice I said, "I'll be back." I took as much stuff as I could handle, risked life, limb, and luggage crossing the main road and struggled up the steep driveway to the hotel. I had no problem securing a room at a rate that was $75 less than I paid with an advance reservation before the trip. I guess it pays to be a walk-in. I took my cargo up to the room and immediately called Ryan's answering machine to leave our hotel phone number. It only took us one more trip to get the rest of the luggage to the hotel. Shortly after we settled into the room, the phone rang.

I answered. "Hello?"

"Dad?"

"That depends. Who's this?" I said.

"It's Ryan."

"Then yes, I'm Dad. Where are you?"

"I got off to a late start. I'm almost in Connecticut."

I continued to play. "Which side? Massachusetts or New York?"

"Massachusetts."

"How are you going to get to Philadelphia in an hour from there?" I asked.

"I'm going to be late," Ryan admitted.

"Really?"

"I'm sorry," said Ryan.

"Don't worry about it. We're staying here tonight, so just go to your apartment and we'll call you tomorrow morning."

After I let Ryan off the hook, Kris and I went back to McDonald's and ordered lunch. The cashier had to give me my 90 cents change in dimes, as she had no quarters. I forgave the manager. After ten days of gourmet food, my Big Mac tasted foreign—but it went down easily.

Back in the hotel, we noted room service trays from breakfast lining the hallway. Raj would never allow such a thing. In the room, I caught Kris studying my forehead. "You know, your scar *is* kinda sexy." I went to the mirror and examined it. The wound was still visible as an angry scar shaped like an "X." I probably should have received a few stitches after all.

A thought occurred to me. "Hey, Celebrity's logo is an 'X'—I've been branded," I said.

"That's kind of spooky," said Kris.

"Maybe you should just call me Mr. 'X.' Do you think the cruise left its mark on me? Is it a sign?"

"It's definitely one for the Mr. 'X' files," answered Kris.

We slipped into bed and lay perfectly still, but the bed seemed to sway very gently. Eyes closed, we were transported back to *Galaxy* where the seas slowly increased in intensity. We belonged there…

Pictures and other materials to accompany the text of this book are available on the Internet (http://book.chesterh.com).

978-1-58348-488-3
1-58348-488-4

Made in the USA
Middletown, DE
14 December 2015